PRINTED IN SWITZERLAND

WILLY BOLLER

MASTERPIECES
OF THE
JAPANESE COLOR
WOODCUT

COLLECTION W. BOLLER

PHOTOGRAPHS BY R. SPRENG

PUBLISHED BY
BOSTON BOOK & ART SHOP, INC.
BOSTON, MASS.

DISTRIBUTED BY
CROWN PUBLISHERS, INC.
419 FOURTH AVENUE
NEW YORK, N.Y.

CONTENTS AND SUMMARY OF ARTISTS

FOREWORD *Ever since our first acquaintance with the Japanese woodcut in the days of the French impressionists it has been a constant source of inspiration to European artists, representing as
it does a felicitous blend of the refinement and wisdom of an ancient artistic tradition with
an immediate and joyous response to life. Nobility of soul, a natural pleasure in the senses,
a knightly freedom in love, engaging humour—these are some of its charms.*

*How fresh these pictures are! Their delicate bloom is like the fragile wonder of a butterfly's
wing; touch it overmuch and it vanishes. For this reason the author has allowed the artistic
and human interest of the pictures to take precedence over the minutiae of scholarship.*

*The book may be regarded as the outcome of an inner bond of sympathy with the works of
these masters. And since the best understanding comes with love, the author seems supremely
qualified to introduce the reader to this art and the spiritual world it conceals. All the pictures
reproduced here have been taken from the author's own collection, but, so great are its riches,
this does not imply restriction of choice but is rather an assurance that the examples selected
have, through long intimacy, proved to be the most impressive and enduring.*

On behalf of the Publishers. T. Burckhardt.

KANO TANYU (1602–1674). *Horses.* Woodcut reproduction of a Chinese ink painting by the
famous artist, from a book published in his memory in 1674. It contains an essay by Tanyu
on the technique of Chinese ink painting and 44 pictures of horses and storks.
9.5 × 14.7 cm.

To its European discoverers, the Japanese woodcut appeared like some miraculous flower springing rootless from the bosom of the earth. They did not realise that it was the last and most refined offshoot from the ancient stem of Eastern Asiatic art. The woodcut, that late bloom, can be understood only if the elements forming an Eastern Asiatic picture be borne in mind. For this is not simply a picture in the occidental sense; it can also be read like any script. It is no mere coincidence that the peoples of the Far East denote painting and writing by the same word. Chinese writing, with its ancient conceptual symbols, is fundamental to pictorial art. Since time immemorial the Far Eastern peoples have expressed themselves in these signs, combined them to form new concepts, and thought in them. Writing, which is a personal play with these symbols, was once regarded as the supreme form of artistic expression. The scribes, painters and wise men endeavoured sometimes to put their thoughts down on paper by means of character symbols, and at other times by drawing the objects which these symbols denoted. Whether one resorted to characters to express oneself or to objective representation was irrelevant. The task of the painting sage was to intensify that incessant pictorial thinking to its supreme expressiveness. Everything animate or inanimate possessed its appropriate symbolic value. The tendril of the pumpkin is the symbol of endurance, and the bud symbolises the future; the open flower stands for the present, and the fading one for the past. Peach pink is the color of chastity, because the blossom of the peach precedes its leaves. The study of painting is tantamount to the assimilation of certain signs, the validity of which for the objects of the visible world has been established since time immemorial. The artist's eye cannot therefore linger on the accidental surface of things. The symbols are already in existence, and they are as familiar to the artist as the letters of the alphabet. Only his imaginative endowment impresses the stamp of his personality on the pictorial symbols. To paint means to write, to versify, to clothe emotional experiences in visible pictorial forms. What matters to Eastern art is not the external picture of nature with its inexhaustible variety of forms and colors, but the profoundest essence of this nature, its living breath. Such art is almost entirely abstracted from the physical aspect of phenomena, and sublimated to a symbol. Depiction is here equivalent to embodiment in the supreme, absolute form of the sign, as elemental and final. The profounder the artist's thought the more abstract the apparently concrete picture.

The early masters schooled in the Chinese tradition were particularly addicted to this symbolic trend in art. But even among the later masters, however revolutionary, there is hardly one capable of freeing himself wholly from the views so deeply engrained in the people itself. Even Hokusai, in his famous picture *The Wave*, magnificently endeavours to interpret existence through the Symbols of Yin and Yang in conformity to an ancient tradition.

The *Ukiyo* picture is never meant to be naturalistic in our sense. The master never strives to portray a nature assumed to be objective and unchangeable outside man. Though all pictures are carefully contrived and constructed, they do not strike us as deliberate. They belong to a spiritualised nature, a nature so highly rarefied and intensified that the rhythm of the universe pulses in their forms.

That such art should have found the technique of the woodcut most congenial is understandable. The Japanese color woodcut is a painting technique carried out by the painters themselves, and not a process of reproduction. Had it been that, we should have to assume the existence of pictures, similar to the later woodcuts, which served as printers' references for the production of color-blocks. Such pictures, however, have never been found. Moreover, the old Japanese books about woodcut technique are very definite on this point. Thus the Japanese artist does not paint a complete picture but produces a series of color-tone sketches, one sketch for each color, which are sent to the engraver's for processing. The engraver pastes each sketch on a wooden block, after which the white paper is cut away and the colored parts are left, thus yielding one color block. A picture of twenty different colors requires, accordingly, twenty different blocks, and, consequently, twenty separate color drawings from the artist. Not until the printer is in possession of all twenty blocks can he produce the picture. He will apply the appropriate color to each block and print them all consecutively on the same sheet. Only then will emerge the picture that neither the wood engraver nor the printer could visualise in advance. Even the artist himself sees his picture for the first time when it comes from the printer's workshop, just as a composer hears his work for the first time when performed by the orchestra, though he himself has composed it and written the score for each instrument.

In the vast majority of cases suitability for reproduction was naturally the reason for the adoption of this technique. It had, however, other advantages. The subtlest color effects were obtainable by the highly complex process of the colored woodcut and were greatly superior to those of brush painting. A case in point is blind-pressing, the technique of embossing lines and surfaces on the paper so that the picture is created by the play of light and shadow on the reliefs. The colors can be printed into the sunken parts, or the areas printed in color can be raised. The paper is roughened in some places, smoothed in others, covered with metal powder, or patches of it subsequently embossed without color. The artist had to paint a separate sheet for each of these complex manipulations, carrying all the necessary instructions to enable the engraver to produce a block for the particular manipulation. Top-grade woodcut prints, such as the *Surimonos*, cost a small fortune, and the imperial decree which for this very reason later prohibited them is striking proof of this. The technique of the colored woodcut demands separate color-tone pictures which must fit each other to a fraction of a millimeter. This presupposes an artist endowed with extraordinary formal and spatial sense. Subsequent corrections are impossible, as the color-tone sketches are destroyed in the process of engraving the block. It was often years before the printing of pictures requiring fifty or more blocks could be embarked upon. When we read that, three years after delivering to the engraver his original color-tone sketches for a picture, Hokusai was still preparing supplementary sketches although he had no records to refer to, such memory for forms appears to us wellnigh incomprehensible.

The fascination of the color woodcut is in all probability due to the precision of its lines and the clear delineations of its surfaces, as well as to the matchless refinements of its coloring. There can be nothing fortuitous, no imprecision or blurred color. Every line and color surface must be thought out in advance by the artist with no subsequent opportunity for correction. The constraint imposed by the need to determine every detail beforehand involves an obligation to work with the most sober attention; there is no scope for the felicitous accident since the high cost of each woodcut demands the highest concentration.

In the infallibility of such minute formal calculation lies the fascination of the Japanese color woodcut, a fascination and a charm to which the French impressionists succumbed in the past as much as do the artists of today.

Devil. A section of a book illustration, 1582. The book of the ten Princes of Hell is one of the oldest dated woodcut books in Japan, and is probably an imitation of a Chinese work.
19.5 × 13.5 cm.

THE EARLY MASTERS:
IWASA MATABEI

The name of the painter after whom the entire school of woodcut artists is called was Iwasa Matabei, styled Ukiyo-Matabei (1578–1650). He was the first to select the subject-matter for his pictures exclusively from the "eventful world", or the world of daily life, *Ukiyo* in Japanese.

Born as the son of the nobleman Araki Murashige from Atami, in Settsu, he was employed in the service of the lords of Fukui, in Echizen, and died on April 22, 1650, at the court of Iyemitsu. The pen-name Matabei is arbitrary. The *Ukiyo-e* school founded by Matabei is a school of painting, and it is probable that Matabei himself did not draw for woodcuts. The only book of woodcuts attributed to him, the "Thirty-six Poetesses", must be regarded as a memorial edition of his drawings.

Despite the established view to the contrary it may be of some significance that *Ukiyo-e* painting did not spring from the poorer classes, but originated among the nobility. Matabei painted his scenes from daily life for aristocratic society. His call to the Court of Iyemitsu, where he painted, among other things, folding screens for the bridal trousseau of Princess Chiyohime, also points to this fact. That the later woodcut artists selected their themes from the *Ukiyo*, the world of the present, was due to the trends then prevalent; they would have conformed as easily to any other fashion of the day.

Iwasa Matabei the son carried on his father's school and published under the name of Matabei II a series of single drawings and woodcut books.

During the "Kiyoho" period, 1716–35, there lived in Otsu a painter they called "Otsu Matahei". The real name of Otsu Matahei was Kyukichi, and he was the most popular painter of the Ukiyo. His paintings, which were inscribed with wise sayings in the manner of votive pictures, were originally religious in content. Later they featured personages from legend and history. Figures like the warrior "Benkei", the man with the falcon, the devil with the lantern, the maiden Fouji and the lance-bearer are found repeatedly and formed popular woodcut themes for more than a century.

As early as the 18th century a host of legends had been woven about the two Matabei and Matahei, who were often mistaken for one another. However, it is certain that they enriched Japanese painting, and thus the art of the woodcut, with new themes.

In the days of the Matabei the woodcut technique was already a thousand years old. The oldest dated woodcut, a "Lion-picture", dates back to the year 740 A.D.

On the right: MATAHEI from Otsu. *Nobleman with a falcon.* Painting on paper. The figure is painted with a few strokes on a coffee-brown chalk ground. The lower part of the garment is bright orange, the trousers olive, the sash rust red, the ground of the overcoat and the falcon grey, both painted over with Chinese ink and white color. Face, hand and feet are heightened with white. 65 × 25 cm.

MORONOBU. An illustrated page from the "Ise Monogatari", illustrated afresh by Moronobu in 1669, and published by Yamamoto Kueimon. The Ise novel, the first illustrated edition of which appeared in 1608, is a collection of 125 anecdotes concerning the Poet-Prince Ariwara no Narihira, the Japanese Don Juan, and was a very popular book. There is hardly one Ukiyo master who did not try his hand at it. The page contains two scenes which in the earlier editions appeared on two separate pages. The top scene, with the inscription *Province of Koochi*, shows the Prince saying farewell to a beloved lady of the Court; the cock on the fence indicates the morning hour. The bottom scene shows two girls at a well, and bears the inscription *Okayasu in the Koochi Province.* 22.5 × 16.5 cm.

旅雁

14

Originally small stamp prints, they were followed in steady evolution by more richly elaborated drawings, writings, texts, books, illustrated books, and single pictures intended to replace paintings. As the fastidiousness of the Edo middle-classes developed along with their increasing wealth during the 17th century, so the quality of the book craft improved. Whereas previously only books of a religious or scientific nature were printed in Kyoto and Osaka, now light literature, too, was printed at Edo, and publishers were forced to provide woodcuts for book illustrations previously painted by hand.

HISHIKAWA MORONOBU
(1625–1694)

Hishikawa Moronobu was born in Hota, Province of Awa. He died a monk at Edo in 1694. As son of an embroidery artist he first followed his father's vocation, learned subsequently to draw and to paint, and produced his woodcuts in the Yamato style, the "style of the Eastland", as opposed to Chinese art, hitherto the accepted ideal. Moronobu is regarded as a national innovator, having by his single prints, albums and books given the people access to an art previously open only to the privileged classes.

Book illustration in woodcut form does not, as is usually assumed, derive purely from Moronobu. He introduced it into Edo, but it had flourished in Kyoto and Osaka for over a century. His illustrated books were not only a magnificent artistic achievement; they were also a novelty to the people of Edo. Various illustrated editions of such books as *Ise monagatari* had already existed for about a hundred years; but only as prized and carefully guarded possessions in the houses and castles of Kyoto's noblemen. Now the treasures of ancient art and literature suddenly found their way, through the woodcut, to the people. It is therefore understandable that the people regarded Moronobu not merely as the artist who introduced them to this novel art form but as its actual inventor.

Moronobu's versatility was unique. Faithful to the *Ukiyo* tradition he found his subject-matter in life as it was lived round him. While the Matabei represented Court scenes, Moronobu painted street scenes, pedlars, and the motley crowd. It was he who published plant and animal books, depicting with convincing realism the predatory tiger in the undergrowth, the hunting weasel carrying off a bird in its jaws, or a cat licking itself.

His illustrated works, numbering over a hundred, unfold a vast panorama of the culture and life of those days. Viewing each picture we experience his spontaneous delight in painting and his susceptibility to the beauty behind all reality. The same artistic sensitivity is evident whatever the subject—whether the movements of a leopard, or the tender beauty of a young girl. Moronobu himself wrote the texts to many of these books—among them the "Sparrows of Edo", which appeared in 1677. Books of drawings, like the fan-decorations of 1682, "Rocks and Trees in the old and new Style" of 1683, or poetry volumes like "The Songs of Yoshiwara" of 1659 were produced. He illustrated afresh the *Ise monogatari*, the 125 anecdotes of Prince Ariwara no Narihira, many editions of which already existed, and so one work illustrating the aspects of the "world in movement" succeeded another.

Picture on the left: *Wild Goose in Flight* (this is what the inscription in the left-hand upper corner means). A woodcut reproduction of a painting in Chinese ink from a book published about 1740 under the title "Ehon umpitsu sogwa" = "Brush strokes" by the famous woodcut artist Tachibana Morikuni (1679–1748). The picture is an example of the wood engravers' craftsmanship, which enabled them to transfer to the woodblock every brushstroke and every color tone with the greatest precision. They thus preserved for posterity thousands of magnificent Chinese ink paintings, the originals of which have long since been destroyed by weather, fire and earthquakes.

21.5 × 32 cm.

In Moronobu's work, too, the *Shunga*, the books devoted to love- and sex life, play an important part. Detached from his subject-matter, he treats this in a natural manner entirely unknown among Europeans. Nowhere is Moronobu so great as in these erotic day-dreams in which he gives his healthy and inexhaustible imagination free rein. The unusual attitude of the Japanese towards the erotic book is illustrated by the fact that Moronobu, who also called himself Kichibei, still continued the publication of *Shunga* after his entry into a monastery. In a preface to an erotic book published at the end of 1694 the publishers Matsu state: "We in no way apologize for concluding with the present *Shunga*, 'Goreiko', the publication of brushworks by the painter called Kichibei of the Hishikawa family."
Moronobu left behind many pupils, the Hishikawa Clan, headed by his son Moronaga, the Ishikawa Clan, headed by Toshiyuki, and the Furuyama Clan under Moroshige. All of them were mainly book illustrators like their master.

In early days single pictures were used mainly for publicity. Although the monasteries and temples were the first to commission them for propaganda purposes, they were subsequently followed by theatre directors, who used these pictures as placards and also as publicity material for their actors. Most orders, however, came from the Yoshiwara-house proprietors, who commissioned from the popular artists this kind of publicity for their Oiran. It is with these single pictures, the publicity pictures, that the woodcut was born as a free, independent form of art.

MORONOBU. From a series of six Court scenes: The *Bugaku*, a ritual dance introduced during the sixth century from Indo-China, is being performed on a raised dais in the open. A lady, accompanied by her maids, lifts a curtain to admire the spectacle. The common folk in the street, seen drinking tea in the bottom right hand corner, also watch.
25 × 35 cm.

Color print: KIYONOBU. Theatre poster. *Kichijuro Tsutsui dances the spear-dance at the Nakamura Theatre in the spring of 1704.*
The inventor of this quaint female dance was Tatsunosuke Mizuki, who came to Edo in 1691 as one of the first actors to mime women. From that date on every male actor of feminine parts, when passing his test at the Shogunal theatres in Edo, had to perform this dance, which represents the delight of a woman at the cleaning of the house. A contemporary poem by Kikakudo says: "Do you dream of flowers, Tatsunosuke, fluttering butterfly? Everybody dances with spears—no, with duster and polishing cloth—the joy of housecleaning."
54.5 × 30 cm.

京下リ

筒井吉十郎

奥村利信筆

KAIGETSUDO ANDO

After Moronobu there appeared in Edo a painter, or rather a group of painters, who employed the woodcut for the production of large-scale pictures, the Kaigetsudo. Whether the pictures, which bear various signatures, are to be attributed to one or more artists is not known. No one will dispute, however, that the 39 famous pictures of courtesans are among the very finest artistic creations of those days. In their solemn serenity these *oiran* are like madonnas rather than courtesans. Never since has any woodcut master created a feminine type of such magnificence and dignity.

The latest research suggests that the pictures are the work of one painter who used various names, as later became the common practice with many artists. Kaigetsudo Ando is probably to be identified with Kaigetsudo Doshin, Kaigetsudo Dohan and Kaigetsudo Anchi, who were formerly thought to be his pupils.

He flourished in the years 1704 to 1716. Ando, whose real name was Genkichi Okazaki, was resident at Kuramaye Asakusa in the Edo business quarter. The Kaigetsudo courtesan pictures remained an inspiration to coming generations of artists and the older Torii in particular were influenced by their genius.

TORII I. KIYONOBU
(1663-1729)

The designation *Torii* appears repeatedly among the confusing clan names at the end of the 17th century. *Torii*, meaning "birdhouse", is the Japanese word for the detached wooden arches which serve to announce to pilgrims the proximity of Shinto temples. The expression *Torii*, as the name of a family of painters, later became a form of honorary title which could be conferred or inherited. Thus the actor and sculptor Soshichi, from Osaka, the inventor of the "forehead cap" for male performers of female parts, styled himself as a painter Torii Kiyomoto, while his son described himself as "the first Torii Kiyonobu".

When the painter Kiyonobu came with his father to Edo in 1687, the books of Moronobu were the fashion of the day. In Danjuro, the greatest actor Japan ever possessed, Edo had a brilliant star. The first *Torii* drew pictures of this popular actor in his roles, thus becoming the creator of actor portraiture, a form which predominated in the woodcut for a century.

Kiyonobu, as head of the Torii group, founded a school of his own, which above all supplied the theatre with posters and portraits of actors. For the next two hundred years this special branch of graphic art remained the prerogative of the *Torii*.

Kiyonobu's pictures do not differentiate between the actor and his part. The actor is hero, demi-god, demon. The symbol-laden masks of the No-dancers come to life in the rigid painted faces. Each movement has its significance and attains in the picture a concentrated and perceptible form. The actor portraiture of the early masters is the ultimate and most precise interpretation of the part, and not merely the portrait of a mime.

After 1703 Kiyonobu enlivened his pictures by painting them over with *tan*, a kind of vermilion. Later he added yellow sap, and frequently a sprinkling of powdered gold. Kiyonobu I and Kiyonobu II are often barely distinguishable in their work, so that it is not certain whether Kiyonobu I is entitled to priority for the *Urushi* picture. Evidence of the epoch-making innovation of mixing glue with black paint to produce a glossy lacquer called Urushi-e can be found in Kiyonobu pictures. The later Torii masters never attained as high a level of actor portraiture as the creator of the first pictures of this genre, Kiyonobu I. Kiyonobu died on July 28, 1729, and was laid to rest in the Seijo-Temple in Edo Asakusa.

Picture p. 17: MASANOBU. *The actor "Sodezaki Miwano" as a girl tying her obi.* On grey paper. The lower part of the garment in bright Beni red, the upper part yellowish. The Obi, in Urushi print with a dark brown pattern, gives the effect of heavy velvet. The calabash in the stamp, the contents of which are mentioned on p. 20, is painted red.
34 × 16 cm.

Picture on the left: OKUMURA TOSHINOBU. floruit 1725-1750, renowned for his hand-colored actor portraits in the Hoso-e format. The actor Nakayama Tomisaburo as flower girl. A print painted over with Beni, yellow, blue, and brown. Signed: Okumura Toshinobu hitsu. Publisher: Hammoto Igeya, Edo.
32 × 15.5 cm.

KAIGETSUDO. *Courtesan*, 1714.
Signed: Nippon Gigwa Kaigetsudo Matsuyo Doshin zu. Stamp-
ed: Doshin. Publisher: Nakaya
Torisaburo-cho.
61 × 28 cm.

NISHIKAWA SUKENOBU
(1671–1751)

The painter who styled himself Nishikawa Sukenobu, a descendant of the Fujiwara family, was, apart from Moronobu, Japan's most popular illustrator. He was and remained throughout his life the child of a big city, a son of the Imperial City of Kyoto. Neither there nor in Osaka did the color woodcut thrive. It was in Edo, the residence of the Shogun, that it attained the rank of an independent art form. Moronobu had transplanted the art of book illustration from its old home in Kyoto to Edo, and when Sukenobu published his first book in black and white in Kyoto, Edo was already familiar with the two-color print. The books of the prolific Master of Kyoto—he published over 300—appeared partly in Edo. There they not only stimulated the early woodcut artists but also served as a model and basis for the artists of the full-color print, such as Harunobu.

The books of Sukenobu are superb *Ukiyo*. In the preface to the *Ehon-Yamato-Hiji*, a picture book with poems, songs, landscapes and scenes from everyday life, Suke-nobu writes: "This is the reason why this little book has been named after our Fatherland. It will present beautiful landscapes to the reader; poets of great force, and departed geniuses. But it will also portray the people and depict various old customs and habits. Hence the name *Yamato Hiji* (Japanese Medley)."

Sukenobu's books are a mine of information for the student of Japanese life of the late 17th century. A born painter, he enriched graphic art in more than one respect. In some ways his black-and-white prints anticipate Harunobu's colored works. Sukenobu was regarded as a great *Shunga* painter, and his *Shunga* pictures achieved

Woodcut above: MASANOBU. From the series "Life in the Yoshiwara". *Oiran in the baths*. A black-and-white print showing Masanobu's femi-nine type at its best.
28 × 37.5 cm.

such popularity that in November 1722 the Government prohibited their publication. This resulted merely in Sukenobu omitting his full signature and continuing his lucrative occupation under a pseudonym. The single sheet color prints sold today are chiefly leaves from books reprinted in Edo during the 19th century. Original printed single sheet Sukenobu pictures have never existed. His great tradition was carried on by a wide circle of disciples headed by his son Tokuyusai, born in 1706, who called himself Suketada. Nishikawa Sukenobu died on September 11, 1751, in Kyoto. He was buried on the premises belonging to the Myosen-Temple.

SUKENOBU. *Girl at a Mirror*, woodcut from the third volume of the Ehon toki-wa-gusa of 1731, a collection of pictures showing scenes from the life of women in the Yoshiwara.
In this Yoshiwara girl, dressing her hair elaborarately bevor the mirror, Sukenobu shows his ideal feminine type, somewhat resembling that of Masanobu. The balance and economy of line, reduced to a minimum, make the picture a masterpiece. Publisher: Morita Shotaro.
24 × 17.5 cm.

TORII KIYOHIRO (1718–1776). *Lovers under a blossoming plum tree*. The poem painted on the picture says that the fragrance of the tree in blossom speaks best for his love when the lover allows his beloved to play his flute. The theme is probably borrowed from the Chinese, and refers to Genso, the T'ang Emperor, and his mistress Yokihi.
By an ingenious exploitation of every possible optical effect resulting from the interplay of the various color surfaces, the picture, printed only in green and red, gives the impression of a rich polychrome painting. Only a careful examination reveals that this is a pure Tan-sei.
Signed: Torii Kiyohiro hitsu. Publisher: Maruko.
42 × 29 cm.

24

SUKENOBU. *Mother and Child*. Illustration from volume III of the Ehon toki-wa-gusa (1731). 24 × 17.5 cm.

TORII KIYOHIRO (1718–1776). *Lovers*. Probably a representation of the Prince-Poet Ariwara no Narihira and his mistress, based on the Ise novel. The poem above says that the lovers' hearts incline towards each other like the flowers in the wind in the blossoming meadow around them. A pure Tan-sei-e, a "Red-green-picture".
Signed: Torii Kiyohiro ga. Publisher: Maruko. 39 × 28.5 cm.

"The genuine brush of the Japanese painter Okumura Masanobu. Tori-shio Street, wholesale picture shop. Sale of saffron pictures and illustrated books. The red bottle-gourd seal is enclosed. Okumura."

This is what the seal says on our beautiful portrait of a girl. The author of this original seal text is Okumura Masanobu himself, one of the inventors of the color woodcut. In the Tori-shio Street studio all forms of painting by hand were tried and standardised.

Masanobu himself did not consider the color print a great invention; he carried it out experimentally and as a matter of course like any other form of hand painting. He notes on his seals: "Sale of saffron pictures", whether the red of the saffron plant has been painted or printed on the picture. The two-color print remains for him and for the people a *Beni-e*, i.e. a saffron picture, be the red color, the *Beni*, printed or painted.

The highly gifted color technician and the inspired artist are felicitously combined in Masanobu's forceful nature. The entire evolution of the color woodcut is encompassed in his work.

The *Tan-e*, introduced by Kiyonobu in 1703, is a black print painted by hand with a vermilion known as *Tan*.

The *Urushi-e*, one of the most important technical innovations, is a print in which the black is rendered lacquer-like by means of a glue *(Uikawa)*. "Blind-pressing", i.e. the pressing of deepened lines and surfaces into the limed parts, resulted in an appearance resembling the lacquer painting of the Tosa school.

Masanobu also overlaid the black printed surfaces with gold and silver.

Beni is a crimson extract from the saffron plant. When dried it has a mica-like brilliance. Light *Beni* is pink, and dark *Beni* of a fiery crimson red. Masanobu added *Beni* by painting or printing it on his pictures.

In 1740 red and green were still painted on the pictures. These two-color compositions of the Okumura publishing house enjoyed such wide popularity that it was decided to print the colors instead of painting them on the pictures. In his wholesale picture-shop Masanobu sold painted red-green woodcuts as well as printed red-green woodcuts under the designation of saffron pictures, red generally being the dominating color. The expression *Tan-sei-e*, vermilion red-green pictures, also originated in the *Tori shio-cho* studio. Though it means only "red-green pictures", it is applied to-day to the color woodcut in general.

A publisher's speciality was the overprinting of red and green in order to obtain a third, violet-like color.

The *Uki*-picture, not to be confused with the *Ukiyo*-picture, is an attempt at perspective. Masanobu described this invention of his as the "near-far pictures".

The *Triptych* is a combination of three separate woodcuts forming one complete picture.

The *Hashira-e* or pillar-picture, also called *Hashira-Kakushi-e*, of unusual elongated format later became an art form of its own. Masanobu signs these elongated pictures, subsequently known as *Naga-e*, or "long-picture", with "*Hashira-e-nemoto*", "Hashira-picture-inventor".

The woodcut thus graduated through its various stages of development in Masanobu's studio. He was the most gifted and most versatile of all the early masters. Of a richly endowed nature, he was inexhaustible in inventing new color techniques and in introducing new forms and subjects. But he was first and foremost an artist in the highest sense of the word, and in quality his pictures excel by far those of his contemporaries. He repeatedly changed his signature, overprinting his pictures in the oddest way with admonitions and warnings against fakes, and describing himself as inventor or "source of things"; or writing: "painted with first-rate colors", "genuine", "unique".

In his studio he employed a number of excellent draughtsmen, and it is clear that a great deal of the work leaving his shop was merely signed by him.

But this is of minor importance compared with the enormous output he left behind. He published 140 books, the first when he was only 12 years old. At the age of 13 he published the famous "Guide to the Yoshiwara", which ran into five editions before he was twenty. At 17 he wrote his "Genji Saga", which he published in 17 illustrated volumes. His magnificent pictures mirror contemporary life, history, literature and legend. Nor is the erotic book, the *Shunga*, missing from his work. Fully conscious of his power and stature as an artist, he bestowed his gifts with munificence.

OKUMURA MASANOBU
(1686–1768)

The Tan-e

The Urushi-e

Gold and Silver
The Beni

The color print

The Uki-picture

The Triptych

The Hashira-e

ISHIKAWA TOYONOBU. *A gallant playing ball.* It is interesting to note that by overprinting grey and red Toyonobu attempted in this picture to achieve a fourth color tone for the trousers, in addition to the red of the lower under-garment, the green of the top garment, and the grey of the drawing. Signed: Ishikawa Toyonobu hitsu. Publisher: Urokogata.
39 × 17 cm.

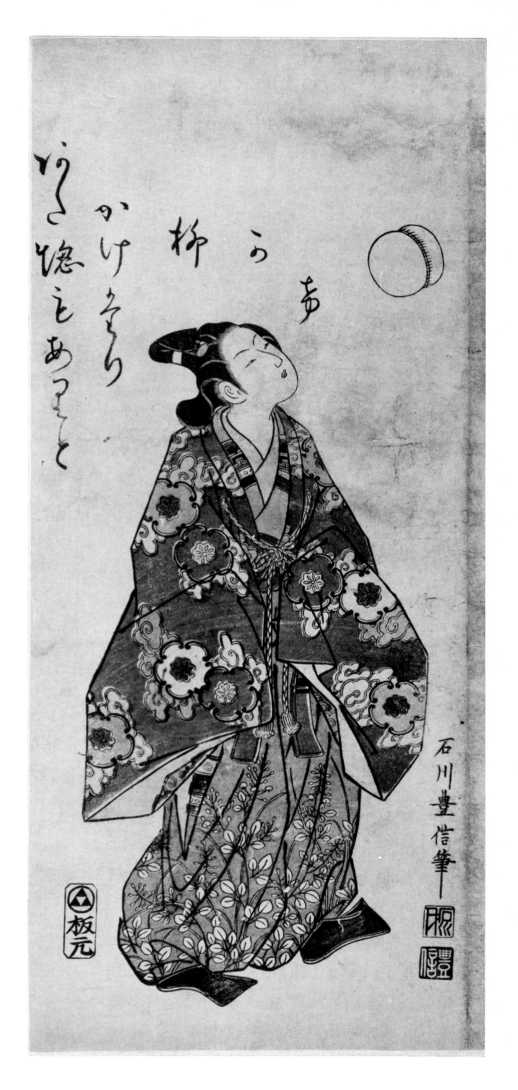

27

哥川 豐峯 画

28

SUZUKI HARUNOBU
(1725–1770)

HARUNOBU. *Beautiful Osen in the Kagiya Inn.* On the side of the lantern is written the name of the tea-house, Kagiya, repeated on the curtain. The inscription on the broad side of the lantern reads: "One may rest here." The picture represents Osen, revered and admired for her beauty and charm, pouring out tea.

Harunobu chose for the picture two different tones of grey, and three different browns. A few details have been executed in blind pressing.

Signed: Harunobu ga.

26 × 18.5 cm.

The charming house of the toothpick merchant Niheiji was situated in the neighborhood of the Kwannon-Temple, in the Asakusa quarter of Edo, in the shadow of an ancient Ginko tree in whose branches white doves cooed. A goldfish pond with a bridge, two cherry trees in blossom and a heavy, crude stone lantern formed the perfect setting for Niheiji's lovely daughter, Ofuji, whose far-famed beauty was the greatest attraction of the toothpick shop. As a seller of toothpicks of the finest bilberry wood, of perfumes and cosmetics, she was already desirably sophisticated and accomplished, despite her tender sixteen years. The elegant customer, however, in whose sake bowl her nimble fingers strewed blossoms, was Harunobu, the painter. Ofuji was his most cherished model. To paint her only as an advertisement for the toothpick shop was not enough; he wished her to grace many of his future pictures.

Harunobu had previously been in love with another model, another sixteen year-old girl, in whom the painter, avid for beauty, saw the acme of feminine perfection. Her name was Osen. Pilgrims flocked to the Kagi house near the Inari shrine, where she served tea, to look at her. Her incomparable beauty was as famous as her virtue. Although a simple country girl, born in 1752 on a farm in Tabatamura, she was highly educated. The people of her time revered her as a paragon of all the feminine qualities. Songs celebrated not only the charm of her movements and the sweetness of her voice, but also her unselfishness and her filial devotion. It seemed as if heaven had showered all its gifts upon her. She herself believed in her beauty as in a kind of bequest from above, and lost nothing of her simplicity when she had to pose as a model for sacrificial puppets for the Buddha feast in Jida. "She bore the beauty of her body and of her soul with dignity." In her own songs, which were on everybody's lips, she admired herself with a delightful naiveté:

At the tea-filled kettle she sits,
She musing, musing all alone
Thinks of this, and thinks of that
And with the silver pin she parts her hair.
He who wishes his limbs to stretch
For a brief span of time
Should rest at Kasamori
In the shadow of a tree.

Osen. 1769

From violet colored vapour clouds
She descends, as were she wholly
In gold and silver lacquer painted.
And he who in the Higurashi village
The wonderful flower beholds
Forgets that from the fifth circle
Of heaven she, like an angel, fell,
Forgets even the glowing fire of hell.

Osen. 1769
(From Kurth, "Japanese Lyrics")

Admittedly, other women also served as models for Harunobu's pictures; among them Ofude from the Hayashi tea-house in Yamashita, and the famous Hinazuru from the Choji-house of the Yoshiwara. Nevertheless it was Osen of Kasamari in whom he found his ideal of chaste girlhood.

To choose the living idol of the people as his model, thus transplanting into the *Ukiyo* and into contemporary life the artistic tradition, which had ossified into the classical forms of the Kano and Tosa schools, may have had a special appeal for the aristocrat Harunobu. But only a very great master could possess the audacity

Confucius riding a mule, from a volume of reproductions of old Sino-Japanese paintings in Chinese ink, published in Japan about 1760.
21.5 × 16 cm.

HARUNOBU. *Girl at the waterfall.* Symbolizes the Chinese sage Hsuyu, who fled into the mountains and washed his ears at the waterfall when he heard that the Emperor wanted to give him the Empire.
Signed: Suzuki Harunobu ga.
27.5 × 21.2 cm.

and skill requisite to embody the old ideas of heaven and hell, the heroes of history and legend in the shape of a widely known young woman of the day.

What we love in Harunobu's girl portraits is their beauty, their grace, and their naiveté. The master himself, however, chose to portray his heroine in the spring of her life for another reason—the opportunity it afforded to evoke legend and history in the form of a concrete and immediate reality. This tender age suited his purpose best because, though still wrapt in dreams, it already yearns for life; though still at home in the realms of poetry, it already belongs to reality. However convincing and genuine Harunobu's prototype may appear in the manifold roles in which he portrayed her, she is at the same time the incarnation of an old tradition; she links past and present—legend and history, gods and saints, fools and sages. Her graceful shape encompasses them all. Even the landscape or any other

HARUNOBU. Full page illustration from the book Yoshiwara Bijin Awase, "Yoshiwara Beauties Collection", black-and-white edition of 1770, Edo, published by Maru-ya Jimpachi.

The book shows on each page a figure, flanked by a poem as decoration. The shape of the written sentence is in harmony with the figure's movement. The gesture of putting the corner of her scarf into her mouth indicates a girl's shyness. The name of this girl is Susono. The short poem reads: "How beautiful now, in the autumn, would be the varied colors of the mountains in my country." Wonderful the formal unison of writing and image, the essential unity of poem and picture.

21.5 × 14.5 cm.

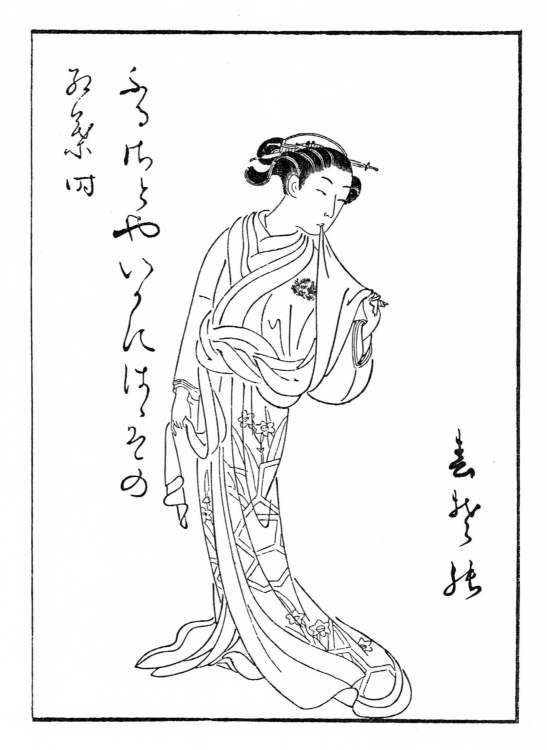

environment in which Harunobu places his heroine—a garden, a room, the banks
of a brook—these are never completely real, they still belong to the fairy world
of children's dreams.

Harunobu does not name his pictures. Following an established Chinese tradition
he leaves it to the onlooker to read into them as much as his education and his
intellectual and emotional development will permit. That well-known little scene
of a girl standing in deep snow and unearthing bamboo shoots—masterly in its
composition and color, and touching, too, in the helplessness with which the
tender child, shivering with cold, wields the wooden pick—evokes an immediate
and general sentimental reponse. The onlooker versed in Far Eastern literature
will, moreover, notice at the first glance that it also represents one of the "Twenty-
four precious stones of child love". If familiar with the significance of the forms

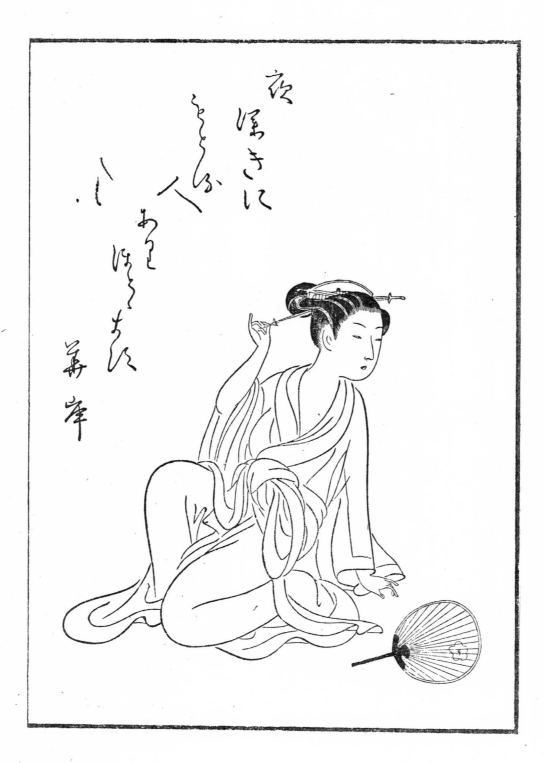

Full page illustration from the book Yoshiwara
Bijin Awase. The short poem reads:

"Is it a visitor who knocks at the door,
So deep in the night?
Is it the voice of the cuckoo?"   (Zengan)

The girl seems to have awakened from a dream.
The fan by her side bears the mark of the Yoshiwara house.
21.5 × 14.5 cm.

HARUNOBU. The picture burlesques the Poet
Prince "Narihira", who admires Fujiyama near
Taga no Ura. The Fuji, the clouds, and the
horse's mane are executed in relief pressing.
Signed: Suzuki Harunobu ga.
28 × 21.5 cm.

鈴木春信画

ISODA KORYUSAI

Mystery still surrounds the painter who describes himself on his woodcuts as "the anchorite-Samurai of Yagenbori at Edo". An inscription on one of his paintings says: *Jikiso*, "presented at Court". He himself prefixes his signature with *Hokkyo*, an honorary title bestowed upon priests. Who was the great master of whose friendship even a Harunobu boasted? We must confess our ignorance.

All we know is that Koryusai worked as a woodcut master from 1765-1780 and as a painter from 1780-1788.

His position in contemporary art is indicated by the fact that he could compete with a Harunobu, whose fame and popularity were unlimited—and that he acquired, moreover, honorary titles denied even to his friend.

The former Samurai of the Daimyo Tsuchiya, whom we rediscover in the Yagenbori, in Edo, after he had left his master and had become a Ronin, was called Isoda Shobei. That is the only certain fact about his life.

Whatever else his biographies record can be no more than guesswork and assumption. Certain only is the quality of his magnificent work which mirrors perhaps more truly than that of Harunobu the age of transition in which the Shogun Tokugawa Yoshimune strove to restore the people's rights and to establish a peaceful state; for Koryusai was himself a Ronin, a discharged mercenary. A young man of those days knew nothing of the battles his forebears had fought, the two swords possessed only decorative value in his eyes, and the women had entirely forgotten that their grandmothers had once ridden on small horses through the steppes. The heroic age had ended, and men everywhere delighted in the beauties of nature, in the chirping of the cricket, the song of the nightingale, and the lovely Yoshiwara girls.

Harunobu developed into a perfect lyrical poet. Not so Koryusai. He, too, strove towards it, but his works are penetrated by a force stronger than the inherited tradition. A glance at his animal pictures—the cat at the fishbowl, the white cock in moonlight, his tiger—proves this. How could the historians believe, as they did for a whole century, Harunobu and Koryusai to be the same artist? Harunobu's animals are the very essence of kindness and gentleness, whereas Koryusai's quiver with force and wildness. The white cat is an enraged beast of prey threatening the onlooker himself, the white cock with his open beak and dilated eyes is about to swoop, the tiger is a savage beast. Yet, despite this, or perhaps because of it, Koryusai's animal pictures are among the most magnificent achievements of Japanese colored graphic art.

Koryusai often resorts to the small size preferred by Harunobu, but he gives his best in the *Hashira-e*, the elongated pictures. Two-thirds of all existing pictures of this type are attributed to Koryusai. He remains matchless in this form, which seems so alien to us and makes such exacting demands on an artist's draughtsmanship and sense of composition. Into this oddly shaped framework of 12 cm. by 70 cm. he fitted legendary and historical figures, *oiran*, lovers, nude studies, and the "Dreams".

In his dream pictures the dreaming woman sits below, while the dream scene is shown above, in a cloud rising from her heart. Koryusai did not paint actors, but produced instead many series of Yoshiwara scenes and *Shungas*. There are no books that can be definitely attributed to him. The single print was his main work.

His coloring differs fundamentally from that of Harunobu, though both masters worked in polychrome. The deep tones in Koryusai's pictures are achieved mainly by the use of orange, of a *Beni*-red (carmine), and a broken blue, combined with heavy black surfaces.

His ideal feminine type is reminiscent of Moronobu's women; the hair style with the protruding wings are Koryusai's own invention, and it is apparent where Kiyonaga found his models.

Extensive use was made of blind pressing and certain parts of his pictures, as for example the plumage of a bird or a white dress, bear no outline, being given their form by this process alone.

Koryusai's pictures are widely scattered. Of his personality or his life nothing is known. Only the remnants of his work bear testimony to his existence; yet the little there is left qualifies him decisively for a place among the greatest masters of the woodcut.

KORYUSAI. *Tiger*. Koryusai expresses his vision of the tiger with unparalleled force. Though printed in monochrome, namely grey, the beast's coat shines and his eyes gleam. As if there were not savageness enough already, the Chinese poem in the picture reads:

"Slept off his blood debauch in the ravine of the mountain.
The vapor of the flesh colors the outskirts of the wood.
Now he has risen, licks his jaws, and enjoys again the remnants of his repast."

Signed: Hokkyo Koryu, mosha kata.
33 × 24.5 cm.

KORYUSAI. *Cat at the Fishbowl*. Silent, tense, the white house-cat puts a paw into the fish bowl. The shining white of the cat's fur stands out against the grey, yellow and copper-red colors of the background.
Signed: Koryusai ga.
26 × 19.4 cm.

From the Harunobu circle. *The Chinese ink sketch of a Kwannon*, from a collection of 1775, is attributed to the Harunobu circle. (The Kwannon is the Goddess of Pity and Mercy, the Bodhisattva Avalokitesvara, represented in Eastern Asia in female form.)
Actual size.

KORYUSAI. *White Cock*. The red sun breaks forth from dark fog and clouds, throwing a mild light on to the foreground. With open beak and eyes dilated the white cock hovers above the unfolding flower. The whole composition is symbolic, each line and color bearing a concealed meaning which eludes, yet holds us spellbound. A unique tricolor print, as the cock's plumage is not outlined, but indicated merely by blind-pressing.
Signed: Koryusai zu.
26 × 19 cm.

From Harunobu's circle. *The Yoshiwara girl* making music is a Chinese ink painting attributed to Harunobu. The girl's features are of a type characteristic of the early master.
Actual size.

KORYUSAI. From the series: Hinagata wakana no hatsu moyo. *First color patterns designed for the young green.*
A famous Oiran of the Yoshiwara and her Kaburo display spring dresses. The Oiran Wakamatsu from the Kadotama-house with her Kaburo plays the zither. The little kneeling Kaburo has the Tsuru (crane) -Mon on her dress. Tricolor print in pink, grey and yellow.
Signed: Koryu ga. Publisher: Eijudo, Edo, 1778.
37.5 × 25 cm.

TACHIBANA MINKO (born 1735). *The Mirror Grinder*. Part of a colored illustrated page from the Shokunin burui, published by Uyemura Tozaburo in 1770. The plates from this magnificent book, one of the first to be printed in polychrome, were destroyed by a fire in 1772. A new edition appeared in 1773, but it lacked the finesse of the first edition, which was printed in very delicate colors. 20.5 × 16 cm.

KORYUSAI. From the series *First Color Patterns Designed for the Young Green*. The Oiran Manzan from the Choji-ya with her two Kaburo and a manservant. Red undergarment, violet top garment, black coat with a green bamboo pattern give this robust peasant girl an elegant appearance. The Kaburo in their violet dresses and the servant in his blue attire heighten the impression of pretended nobility.
Signed: Koryusai ga. Relief pressing from the Eijudo Publishing House, 1770.
38 × 26 cm.

Horses. A page from the book "Japanese and Chinese master drawings", with reproductions of old Chinese ink drawings, published in Japan in 1752. 20.5 × 15.5 cm.

KORYUSAI. From the great series: *First Color Patterns Designed for the Young Green*. In the company of her Kaburo, a famous Oiran displays the spring dresses. The Oiran Tamatsusa from the Yada-house with two Kaburo, one of whom carries a cage. The mistress and her servants wear the same grey-violet coats with a wave-like pattern, while top and undergarments are in two shades of pink. The three girls look very much alike and probably represent the urban type of beauty.
Signed: Koryusai ga. Publisher: Eijudo, Edo, 1778. 39 × 26.5 cm.

KATSUKAWA SHUNSHO
(1726–1792)

The Katsukawa school was named after the birthplace of its master Shunsho, whose real name was Yusuke, and who was supposed to be a descendant of the noble Fujiwara line, born in Kachigawa—"Katsukawa" in the Edo dialect— in the Province of Owari.

This poor artist, who for years was engaged in producing actors' portraits for his master Shichiyemon on Ningyo street in Edo in return for board and lodgings, had, at the age of 42, a sudden stroke of luck. The actors' portraits he had drawn for the Kabuki plays performed in 1768 at the Nakamura Theatre were so eagerly bought that Shunsho became famous overnight.

Two years later he published together with Buncho the famous *Ehon Butai Ogi*, the "Fan book", which shows on white fans the colored half-length portraits of Edo's most popular actors against a blue background. As the first book of color-printed actor portraits it represents a document of fundamental importance not only for the history of the Japanese theatre but also for the history of actor portraiture. And if the publishers Kariganeya Ihei gave the Sembu shukuen, the "Thousand Prints Feast", in honour of the two artists—a feast that went down in history— it was not without very good reason; Shunsho's art had made them a fortune. Though Shunsho's book carried on the old Torii tradition of actor portraiture, which Harunobu's brilliant artistry had temporarily suspended, it differs from the old Torii in its more realistic approach. It is impossible to mistake the face of a Danjuro for that of a Koshiro, even when both are represented in the same role. These pictures are still determined by tradition, their forms and surfaces still have symbolic significance, yet color comes increasingly into its own. Chromatic effects become an end in themselves, thus heralding a period in the history of the Japanese woodcut that has frequently been called classical. It reaches its apogee and finds its consummation in the art of Kiyonaga, the fourth Torii.

Shunsho gave the people actor portraits which combine the characteristics of the actor's individuality with those of his role. Yet, however individual in appearance, these portraits contain no other features than those inherent in the actor's performance. For in private life Shunsho was loath to mix with the "rabble" of actors, and outside his artistic duties made a point of dissociating himself from them. In his preface to the book *Yakusha natsu no Fuji*—the title of which, meaning "The actor as summer Fuji", alludes to the actor without grease-paint and compares him to the Fuji in the summer bereft of its majestic snow cap—Shunsho publicly repudiates any suspicion of social intercourse with these people. He writes: "... Year after year, in one year as in the following, the flowers are alike; but year after year, in one year as in the next, the pictures which the figures of the drama commit to the much coveted print are dissimilar, whether they are painted in vermilion and green, in saffron and indigo, whether strong or light in color. I have let myself be persuaded to illustrate the *Tsusho*, and to represent the mimes in their everyday appearance, which means with their real faces. Yet though I of course love the theatre and rejoice to attend it I have no dealings with the actors themselves and do not know them in their private lives. Therefore, being unable to paint their real features, their unpowdered faces, I should have declined. Yet even though there be little resemblance, it may still be a pleasant way of beguiling time. And so I yielded to the insistent demands.

Anei 9. Year of the Mouse, in the winter. Katsukawa Shunsho."

If it is true that Shunsho was a descendant of the proud Fujiwara, this preface is quite understandable.

Shunsho's art is by no means limited to the portrayal of actors. His *Ise Monogatari*, in the style of Harunobu, published 1772, shows him to be a master of illustration; the same applies to his book on silkworm culture, in the same style, which appeared in 1776. Shunsho frequently, and willingly, cooperated with other artists in producing a joint work; together with Buncho, born in 1723, he painted the "Fan-book" and many *Shunga;* and in collaboration with Kitao Shigemasa, in 1776, published the "Mirror of Beautiful Women of the Green Houses".

In this last work, which is their most important and most handsome, the two artists endeavoured, like all other masters of the Tokugawa epoch, to evolve the prototype of the ideal Japanese woman. For this purpose they chose the Yoshiwara, the mirror of Japanese womanhood, as their model. The pictures of the book are arranged in the order of the seasons, and relate to the feasts and symbolic plants of the months; chrysanthemums blossom in November, windflowers in June, peonies in May. Among the feasts represented are the contemplation of the moon, the February puppet feast, and the Tana-bata feast in August; we observe the beauties at play and making music, enjoying archery or otherwise beguiling their time. But however pretty and happy this new feminine type, it was left to Kiyonaga, who took this book and Koryusai's work as his point of departure, to delineate in its final form an ideal which has remained unchallenged in Japan down to the present day.

With the nomination of Kiyonaga to the dignity of the fourth Torii, Shunsho abandoned the woodcut and returned to painting, the art of his forbears. He died on January 19, 1792.

SHUNSHO. *Two peasant girls collecting silkworm eggs.* First page from the Kaiko Yashinai Gusa, 1776, a series of 12 prints devoted to silk-culture.

The original shows a delightful harmony of colors; the floor is bright green, woodwork and sky are grey, the girls' undergarments vermilion and their top garments violet. The beauty of the picture is enhanced by the harmony of the two figures, with their common rhythm of form and color. This is clearly intended to have symbolic meaning.

Signed: Katsukawa Shunsho ga. 26.5 × 19 cm.

SHUNSHO. Uzaemon IX. *The actor Ichimura Uzae-mon IX in the drama "Sakimasuya Mume no Kachi-doki".* As in the Danjuro picture, Shunsho has exaggerated the proportions of the actor's crest so that it becomes the immediate focus of attention. The crest on the curtain is that of the Ichimura Theatre, where Uzaemon performed for more than 50 years. Signed: Shunsho ga. 33 × 14.5 cm.

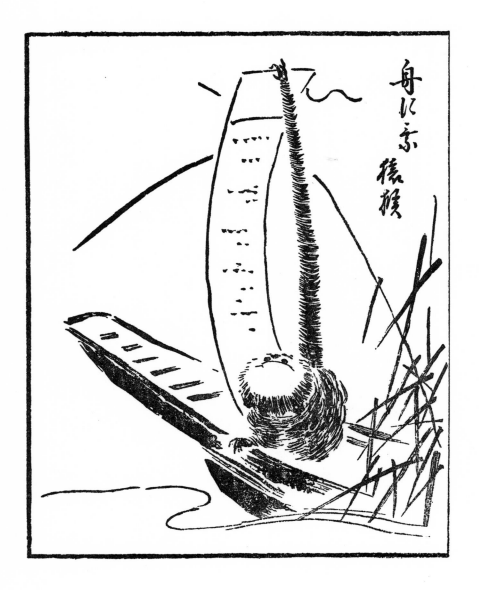

HANABUSA ITCHO (1652–1724). Itcho, who was banished for 12 years to an island as punishment for a humorous picture, carried on with his spirited drawings while in exile. They were all published posthumously in woodcut books. The little monkey which uses a Kakemono as a sail is reproduced from the second volume of the Itcho-gafu, 1770. 20.5 × 15.5 cm.

SHUNSHO. *The Oiran of the Kiri-ya shooting with a bow.* From Seiro Bijin Awase Suguta Kagami, "Mirror of Beautiful Women of the Green Houses", a color book in three volumes by Shunsho and Shigemasa, 1776, which shows the Oiran at her occupations and amusements.
The four-color print with red as its predominant color shows the beauties shooting with the bow. On the right sits the Oiran Kikuzono, next to her Mitsuhana holding the bow, then Toyomachi in the black-patterned coat, and on the left Hanakiri. In this picture we meet for the first time Shunsho's feminine prototype, from which Kyonaga derived his own, the so-called classical type of the Japanese woman.
Publisher: Yamazaki Kimbei, Edo. 21.5 × 30 cm.

THE DISCIPLES OF SHUNSHO

Shunsho's significance for his contemporaries is proved by his pupils Shenei, Shunko, Shuncho, Shunro (Hokusai's name as a pupil), Shunsen, Shunzan, as well as by those artists, such as Utamaro and Toyokuni I, who received their first grounding in the master's studio after his death. Shunei I and Shunko I were the most faithful among his pupils.

KATSUKAWA SHUNEI I
(1762–1819)

SHUNEI. *Actors*. The actor Matsumoto Koshiro standing against a black sky and sitting near him Nakamuro Denkuro II, both in the role of sedan chair carriers.

The dull red and blue tones—Koshiro in a violet coat, Denkuro in a red coat and a bluish garment—enhance the tense atmosphere of this four-color print.

Signed: Shunei ga. Publisher: Eijudo, Edo. 25.5 × 18 cm.

Shunei I, born 1762, was a descendant of the Isoda, from which Koryusai also descended. He was a prodigy, and from his earliest childhood amazed people, including his parents, by his attainments as painter, singer, musician and woodcut artist. He published his first book of woodcuts in 1782 at the age of fourteen.

In his early days he also worked as cartoonist in the tea-house of the Niwaka Theatre, where he painted caricatures of the actors on the promenade fans of the theatre-goers. The style of this type of picture is still described to-day as Kutoku style, derived from his real name Kutokusai. Shunei possessed remarkable talent, far excelling in versatility the teacher of his young days, Shunsho. After Shunsho's retirement he became the spiritus rector of the school, later founding a school of his own, which produced important masters. After Shunsho's death he changed his style, and created the large heads against a mica background which served as models for Sharaku; there are reminiscences of Kiyonaga and Utamaro in his work, especially in the feminine types of his *Shunga*.

Shunei left many pupils who continued his style up to the period of decadence. He died in 1819.

KATSUKAWA SHUNCHO (1772–1800). Page from a Shunga of 1790.
18.2 × 13.8 cm.

SHUNEI. *The actor Osagawa Tsuneyo as a laundress.*
Three-color print in various tones of ochre yellow.
Signed: Shunei ga. In the right upper corner the
collector seal of the Kanesaburo, 1835–1908. Publisher: Tsuruya Kiyeimon.
31.5 × 15.5 cm.

KATSUKAWA SHUNKO I
(died 1827)

Shunko I, whose date of birth we do not know, was called Denjiro. At first he styled himself Shun-o, subsequently Shunko, and from January 19, 1792, the day on which his teacher died, Shunsho II.

His first books appeared in 1780. Like Shunei he has drawn numerous pictures of wrestlers. Later he drew actors-"*hoso-e*", and finally the large heads on colored grounds which he published at the opening of the 1791 spring season of the Nichimura Theatre.

When his right arm became paralysed by a stroke at the age of forty, he retired into the Zenfuku Temple, where he died in 1827.

Woodcut reproduction of a Chinese ink painting, from a volume "Sino-Japanese master pictures", 1760.
21 × 15 cm.

SHUNKO I. *Sakata Hangoro III in the part of Kudo Suketsune* in the drama Haru-no iro Edo-e Soga during its performance at the Ichimura Theatre, in May 1791.
Blue-green ground; blue-green face-paint; yellow color and vermilion-red stripe of undergarment.
Signed: Shunko ga. 38.5 × 25.5 cm.

In 1781 fortune smiled on Hosoda Mizaburo Tokitomi, the chamberlain and court painter of Shogun Iyeharu: his painting of the Sumida river found favour with the Emperor. The picture was acquired for the collection of Emperor Ko-kaku, and from then on the painter used the imprint *Ten-Ran:* "Seen by the Emperor." How and when this distinguished court artist, who signed his pictures with the name "Eishi", took up the art of the woodcut is unknown. We do, how-ever, know that his triptychs illustrating the life of the Prince Genji, and his series of *Ukiyo* pictures of court scenes, were first on sale in 1781. During the 20 years in which Eishi produced woodcuts, in addition to paintings, he made an outstanding and most original contribution to this art form.

His series of separate elongated prints, designed to be combined in sets of six, seven or nine to form a single picture, are very unusual. The entire *Ukiyo* provided him with subject-matter. He represents court and tea-house scenes and historical episodes, and produces numerous series on Yoshiwara themes—for Eishi is pre-eminently a painter of women. He developed a style of his own which betrays his aristocratic origins. The splendours of court life and the aloof nobility of his personality are reflected in his inimitable color compositions. With violet and black, perhaps a touch of grey, he evokes entirely new and solemn moods. He frequently colors the entire background yellowish brown, leaving only a few white surfaces, thus achieving the effect of the old lacquer pictures, an effect en-hanced and completed by gilding the edge of the clouds. Forms and colors are often endowed with a symbolic significance, and almost every picture shows him as belonging to the aristocratic Kano School rooted in Chinese tradition. Above all, however, Eishi is the painter of beautiful women and, whether representing women singly or in groups, at home in the Yoshiwara or in the street, to him a woman is always a tall and slim princess. Her noble reserve is in keeping with the ideal of extreme refinement cultivated in that period. She is the incarnation of the Japanese ideal of propriety, which frowns upon every uninhibited emotional ex-pression as unseemly. If Eishi's forerunners avoided any show of feelings in their indolently moving figures, Eishi freezes the countenance of the Japanese woman to a rigid mask. The coloring is as beautiful and noble as the drawing. All strong tones are excluded, the color symphonies are muted, and the cool harmonies, cre-ated with carmine, green and deep black on a yellow ground, are reminiscent of the violet-brocade pictures.

Twenty-six artists between 1790 and 1800 described themselves in their signa-tures as pupils of Eishi. Strangely enough their activities, too, ended suddenly about 1800, when their master renounced the art of the woodcut to devote himself once more entirely to brush painting. Eishi died in 1829, at the age of 73.

HOSODA EISHI
(1756–1829)

EISHI. From a series of seven full-page drawings under the title *Collection of the Treasures of the Gods of Good Fortune.*
A lady sits before a table with the figure of the crane, supposedly a bird of good omen. The ground of the original is yellow, the lady's dress is white, the Obi orange, the coat pale brown with green designs, the table green, and the comb yellow. All colors are tender and subdued. The picture is very characteristic of Eishi's aristocratic style.
Signed: Eishi zu. Publisher: Eijudo, Edo.
37.5 × 24 cm.

EISHI. *A publicity print for the beauties of the Matsuba house* with the inscription: "Matsuba-ya; one of three prints". The four Oiran, seen from right to left, bear the following poetic names:

Wakakusa	(Young grass shoots)
Aga Tabune	(Little coastal boat)
Matsukaze	(Wind in the pines)
Tomikawa	(Little Tomi river)

The colors of the figures, a wonderful harmony of red and green, are printed in relief-pressing on a yellow ground.
Signed: Eishi ga. Publisher: Eijudo, Edo.
38 × 25 cm.

Color print: EISHI *Takigawa, a beauty from the Ogi house,* from the series: Seiro bisen awase; Selection of Beauties from the Green Houses.
Signed: Eishi ga.
38×25 cm.

Picture p. 81: EISHI. Picture from a series *Furyu shichi Komachi, Amagoi.* Seven elegant modern Komachi, the rain beseechers. Print in various shades of blue and grey.
Signed: Eishi ga. Date 1788. Publisher: Senichi Han. 38×25 cm.

EISHI. The middle part of a triptych, showing ladies on the beach resting on a boat, while the maids and menservants collect shells. The sand is grey, the border of the boat copper red, the wood beneath is yellow. The lady seated on the right wears a pink undergarment, a white collar and a yellow Obi. The maid in a mallow-colored dress, white undergarment and yellow Obi carries an ochre-yellow wooden vessel. The boy's dress is grey. In relief-pressing.
Signed: Eishi ga. 38 × 25 cm.

KITAO MASAYOSHI (1761–1824). From the book Iimbutsu Oyakugwashiki, *Human Portraits*, 1795. The very accomplished draughtsman Masayoshi delighted in parodies of Japanese life and popular motives of Japanese painting, which he collected in a book full of humorous scenes.
21 × 16 cm.

CHOKOSAI EISHO. Eisho (floruit 1780–1800), Eishi's son, gained popularity with his half-length portraits of famous Oiran. A mild, knowing smile glides across the faces of the women he portrays, and comes to rest on their lips. Kasugano from the Sasaya, in a bathrobe with lilac stars, drying the lobe of her right ear. The background is yellowish, the hair-band pink.
Signed: Eisho ga. Publisher: Yamaguchiya Chusuke, Edo. 38.5 × 24.5 cm.

From Masayoshi's *Human Portraits*, 1795: a pilgrim looking at the Fuji, a boy running after an escaped bull (a popular motive), anglers, and a man in a boat.
21 × 16 cm.

EIRI (floruit 1793–1802). *Portrait of Santo Kyoden, poet and painter*. From the series: "The Flowers of Edo."
Signed: Eiri ga. Publisher unknown. 37 × 25.6 cm.

ICHIRAKUTEI EISUI was a pupil of Eishi (floruit 1780 to 1797). Under the title *Beauty of the Joruri* this master painted a series of lovers as represented in the Joruri plays. The print shows the famous Komurasaki with her bridegroom Gompachi bidding her farewell at the entrance to the Yoshiwara house in which he found her.

The ground of the picture is grey. Komurasaki wears a pink undergarment, a white collar and a red dress, a lilac-colored coat and an olive-green Obi. Gompachi wears a black dress with a violet pattern and a yellow hat.

Signed: Ichirakutei Eisui ga. Publisher: Bonjudo. 38 × 24.5 cm.

TORII KIYONAGA
(1752–1815)

Torii Kiyonaga, the son of a tobacco merchant called Seki from Uraga in the Sagami bay, was born in 1752 and named Ichibei. Years later, after the family had left the small port of Uraga for Edo, where they opened a tobacco shop in the Honseimoku Street, we find young Ichibei an efficient businessman. A few more years, and the young tobacco merchant Ichibei Seki was working in the studio of the third Torii Kiyomitsu, producing placards for the theatre of Edo. He now styled himself Sekiguchi or Kiyonaga-Seki. After the death of the third Kiyomitsu his son-in-law Kameji became Torii. But the actors and theatre directors forced him to resign, and Kiyonaga inherited the Torii title.

At that time Koryusai was living in retirement and Shunsho and Toyoharu had returned to classical painting, so that the fourth Torii Kiyonaga suddenly found himself the most prominent exponent of the woodcut art of his day. It is remarkable, however, that he did not achieve greatness by the portrayal of actors, the very craft of the Torii whose title he bore. He won his fame by his portrayal of what is still considered the ideal prototype of Japanese womanhood. Moronobu, Harunobu, Koryusai—each created a distinct feminine type which was esteemed above the prejudices of personal taste. Yet it was Kiyonaga who discovered the enduring ideal. After a century of attempts this race of predominantly squat people, with snub noses in their broad moon-like faces, found the dreamt of feminine ideal in Kiyonaga's tall, noble women, with their refined oval faces and slender limbs. And whereas Moronobu's short feminine figures are painted on a surface without background, and Hanurobu's lovely creatures appear in an environment, which, like the world of a child, consists of unrelated objects, Kiyonaga's mature women are set in a perfect landscape with which they blend in form and essence, in appearance and significance.

How aristocratic is the poise of these women with their tight coiffures! Their gait is regal, their nobility lends elegance even to the maids accompanying them. Deep chromatic harmonies of green, red and black enhance this formally perfect composition. Despite their accomplished virtuosity the pictures are so natural and unconstrained that we might be inclined to regard them solely as the personal inspiration of an artist of genius. But behind Kiyonaga, and behind the masses that understood and acclaimed him, lies the centuries-old tradition of this art, hundreds of years of profound thought, and an infinitely long, patient education of the observing eye and the drawing hand. This wonderful world without shadows, in which man walks with winged steps through the bright light of the day, was never external reality, but always and only inward vision. The beautiful courtesans, the middle-class women, the ladies of the court who populate the pictures were never meant to be merely portraits of contemporary feminine types. Kiyonaga evolved their shapes in long and laborious years, and succeeded in crystallizing in an enduring formula the artistic finds of a century.

Admired by the people and esteemed by the artists, he suddenly abandoned the art of the woodcut in 1790, at the height of his fame. He thought his hour had come; proudly and with royal dignity he renounced his titles and retired. He died 25 years later, in 1815. His work is particularly admired in the Japan of today.

KIYONAGA. *Three women walking along a river bank.* The lady in the centre: violet-blue striped dress with vermilion undergarment and brown Obi. Maid on her right: black Obi, dress white with olive-green pattern. Lady to her left: black dress with yellow pattern, vermilion undergarment, brown and yellow Obi. The river is green-yellow, the sky grey.
Signed: Kiyonaga ga. 37.3 × 24.5 cm.

KIYONAGA. From the series *Fuzoku Azuma no nishi-ki—Modern Eastland Brocade*. Title in the top left-hand corner in Ten script. The lady wears a broad yellow hat and a fan of the same color, a bright pink patterned dress, a vermilion collar, and a yellow Obi.

The two maids accompanying her carry an olive-green parasol. Their dresses are mallow-colored. The background of the picture is grey.

Signed: Kiyonaga ga. 38 × 25 cm.

KIYONAGA. From the series *Fuzoku Azuma no nishi-*
ki—Modern Eastland (Edo) Brocade.
Standing lady drying her ear with her bath-robe.
The sitting maid, in a red-brown dress and a black
Obi, holds a baby whose red dress shows a pattern
of the Danjuro crest. The lady's light-brown bath-
robe shows a rich olive-colored pattern. The ground
is grey.
The indication of the series, at the top, in Ten script.
Period 1784–1785.
Signed: Kiyonaga ga. 37.2 × 24.5 cm.

KIYONAGA. *The actor of feminine parts Segawa Kikunojo III* performs the butterfly dance at the Nakamura Theatre.
Signed: Kiyonaga ga. Publisher: Eijudo.
38 × 25.5 cm.

KIYONAGA. *A mighty warrior throws his treasures to the devils.* Top garment green, trousers light-brown with white pattern. The devils in red robes. Much blind-pressing.
Signed: Kiyonaga ga. Publisher: Eijudo.
38 × 25.6 cm.

On May 3, 1806, there died in Edo, lovingly cared for by his young and pretty wife, but broken in spirit and hard driven to his last breath by his publishers and backers, Japan's great painter of women, Kitagawa Utamaro. He must have welcomed death as a liberator. His life had been consumed in thirty years of restless and passionate work, leaving behind a unique artistic heritage.

His real name was Yusuke Kitagawa; he was born in 1753 in the small town of Kawagoye near Edo. As a young child he came under the tutelage of his later teacher, the Kano-painter, Toriyama Sekiyen, who initiated him in the art of drawing and painting. At seventeen he left the Kano School together with his teacher, and both devoted themselves to the woodcut. The master signed his pictures Toyofusa, the pupil Yusuke as Toyoakira. Though Yusuke became a civil servant, his whole life was dedicated to art. This is the period during which Harunobu died, Shunsho passed the zenith of his career, and Kiyonaga attained a leading position. Yet Toyoakira went his own way. Every book of his, every picture is a milestone on the road of his liberation from teacher and school. He resigned from his position as civil servant and changed his name, calling himself first Murasaki-ya, and subsequently Utamaro. *Uta* means "the song", *maro* "we"—the We used by Kings alone—We, Artist by God's Grace!

Utamaro's art is an impassioned endeavour to record with the brush the beauties of nature. Whether it is the frail structure of a dragon-fly's wing, a tiger's fangs, or the body of a young girl, all are treated with the same care, the same piety, and committed to paper with equal precision of line. "What the heart grasps, the brush reproduces; the painting of my pupil Utamaro is the painting of the heart", writes his teacher introducing his first book, the "Shell-book", published 1780, with which Utamaro became independent. Proudly Utamaro adds to his name, already pretentious enough, the words "Jisei Ikke". (One that has built a house unto himself, i.e. who represents a school of his own.)

The free artistic life was of short duration. Edo's most famous publisher, Tsutaya Jusaburo, discovered him, purchased his entire production, and took him under his roof. The great genius was never to leave Jusaburo's golden cage again. Though he remained the most popular and best paid artist of his day, he was a spendthrift, and his love of luxury made him permanently dependent upon his financial backers. He spent his days in feverish activity in Jusaburo's studio, and the nights in the Yoshiwara, at the gate of which he lived. At the age of 43 he married a young, very talented girl of exceptional beauty who helped him in his work. Disaster befell him at the summit of his career: a very touchy military government took exception to a satirical triptych of his, and Utamaro was sent to prison. This broke his luminous wings; imprisonment finally undermined the health of an already frail body. He died shortly after his release. He was a child of his age; quick ascendancy to fame, excessive work, intensive living, tremendous popularity, and a brutal end at the hands of despots.

Utamaro's work, from the "Shell-book", published 1780, to the "Yearbook of the Green Houses", which appeared in 1804, is a succession of triumphs. His complete works form a colossal collection of over 600 series, books and albums. They represent a unique historical document of the last phase of the Tokugawa Princes. If in his early days Utamaro preferred animals and plants as his themes, after 1790 he shows a definite predilection for the portrayal of women or mothers.

Edmond de Goncourt named his Utamaro biography, published in 1891, "Le peintre des maisons vertes". That Utamaro sought and found the models for his feminine portraits in the Yoshiwara is natural. All woodcut masters had represented the beauties of the "Green Houses". Moronobu, who was later to become a monk, published a guidebook to the Yoshiwara; Masanobu produced "New Pictures of the Yoshiwara Beauties", Harunobu "Yoshiwara Beauties", while Shunsho and Shigemasa's best work bears the title "Mirror of the Beauties of the Green Houses". For Utamaro, however, the brothels were more than mere subjects for a series of pictures—they were the very prerequisite of his art; to him they were life itself.

The Yoshiwara, mirror of Japan, whither the most beautiful girls were brought from all over the land, where the village maidens exchanged their simple garb for court dresses and their rough dialects for the classical language; the Yoshiwara, luxury city with its 3,000 girls, their life governed by a code of their own, by strict ceremonial rules for every occasion, was an enchanted world—"so beautiful and clean that it was difficult to believe one was on this earth", runs a saying

UTAMARO. *A beauty surveys herself in the looking-glass.* The poem likens the shapely line of her throat to the Bay of Sumiyoshi.
Signed: Utamaro hitsu. Publishers: Isemago.
38.5 × 26 cm.

Picture p. 101: UTAMARO. *Yamauba gives the little Kintoki a chestnut to play with.* According to the legend, the hero Kintoki was the servant of Prince Yorimitsu, ancestor of the first Shogun Yoritomo. Kintoki's father had been killed by invading hordes, and his mother Yamauba escaped with her child into the mountain forests where, living on fruits, she brought the child up at her breast.
Yamauba wears a green dress with a pattern of dark green leaves. The undergarment, of which only little can be seen around the naked breasts, is red. Little Kintoki's skin is red-brown, his tonsure bluish. The ground is grey.
Signed: Utamaro hitsu. Publisher: Yohachi.
51 × 22.5 cm.

of the time. The Yoshiwara was the dream of rich and poor, the meeting point of noble and mean, all united by a common instinct and common ceremonies. There they rubbed shoulders, the rice planters visiting the city, and the Daimyo who had come from their castles to bring homage to the Shogun; all had to pass the same gateway, to receive the white kimono which gave them all the same appearance and the same rank.

What extremes of luxury and poverty, of cheerfulness and sadness! What a wealth of romance and intrigue for the observant artist! The Yoshiwara did not even lack a certain nobility of soul. For was it not the residence of the selfless Komurasaki, who had sold herself out of love for her parents? Here her bridegroom found her. Despair drove him into the commission of acts for which he was subsequently executed. Komurasaki fled and committed suicide on her lover's grave. Many poems were composed in their praise. Their legend will live for ever.

The Yoshiwara! What a paradise for an artist like Utamaro! His art is one long paean to the "Green Houses". We find in his pictures the whole hierarchy of the Oiran together with the youthful Shinzo and the youngest of all, the Kaburo, who were scarcely out of childhood. Ippensha Ikku writes in 1803: "The standard of their education approaches that of royal princesses. They learn dancing, painting, classical music and literature, tea ceremonies, the perfume-play, and the thousand things that make a woman lovable."

The very titles which Utamaro chooses for his pictures indicate their narrative nature: "First appearance as singer", "Game of hide-and-seek when the woman-superintendent is away", "The Feast of the White Dresses on August 1st", "Niwaka", "First Meeting", "First Acquaintance", "Mature Acquaintance", "The Evening Meal", "Awakening", "Seeing off to the Stairs", "Farewell". The scenes in the open are also described in such captions as "Oiran visiting each other", "Promenade", "January 2nd", "Night on Middle Street", "The Planting of Cherry Trees", "Masquerade", "Admiring the Moon and the Cherry Blossoms", "Lantern Feast", and so on, one series devoted to Yoshiwara life following another. Harunobu's girls loved the fresh early morning snow, Kiyonaga's women the sunny day, Utamaro's women show a preference for eventide and night, the time of the mosquito nets and the mysterious shadows on the paper walls.

In everything and through everything Utamaro sees Woman, the eternal feminine. The very titles of his series are significant: "The Seven Gods of Happiness represented by Women", "Courtesans Compared to Flowers", "The Six Arms of the Tama River represented by Women", "Snow, Moon and Flowers symbolized by Women", "The 53 Stations (Landscapes) of the Eastern Sea Ways represented by Women". Time and again it is woman that inspires Utamaro to his highest attainment. Whether woman is shown in the rigid court dress or naked in the ecstasy of love the master's great art elevates her to the rank of nature's most perfect creature. Utamaro found in the Yoshiwara all models for his feminine portraits, particularly for his exquisite mother-portraits. Even Yamauba, the accepted prototype of the Japanese hero-mothers, must have been a poor girl from the Northern Provinces who posed as Utamaro's model in a "Green House".

Utamaro's pictures were famous far beyond the frontiers of Japan, and still enjoy great popularity.

The master's personal life has been criticised in Europe by the competent and incompetent alike. The West will always find it difficult to understand the environment in which the great painter was born. Yet the accusation of a useless life can hardly be levelled against a man who accomplished works of such magnitude. A sentence from a letter addressed by his wife to a publisher may be quoted in this connection. In her husband's absence—he was in Enoshima—she had sent the artist's colored drawings for an erotic work to the publishers Matsu-midori-ya, and wrote in her letter: "... Such work is most painful to a woman but I am, after all, the wife of a painter. You may find in the drawings various inexactitudes that will not appeal to you, but you must always bear in mind what a happy couple we are..."

His life blazed and burnt itself out all too quickly, meteorlike. But his artistic inheritance, quantitatively rich and qualitatively superb, testifies to a life of great inward fervour and richness.

We do not know the real life of the Yoshiwara woman. In Utamaro's art she appears as a queen. He painted the women of Japan and of the Yoshiwara as he saw them. And it must be borne in mind that these pictures are not drawn from

UTAMARO. *Yamauba holds her beloved son on her lap.* Yamauba's face is white, her teeth painted black, and she wears a green dress with a leaf pattern. Kintoki, her child, represented as usual with a red-brown skin, wears a black-and-grey checked garment over his sulphur-yellow undergarment. The ground of the picture is grey. Utamaro's conception of both figures has been universally accepted. Signed: Utamaro hitsu. Publisher: Yohachi. 37 × 26 cm. Late print.

memory, but are sketches from life, and may therefore claim resemblance to their models. Often intended as publicity for the girls, they bear their names and the names of the "Green House" in which they lived.

Utamaro's Yoshiwara became the idol of the Tokugawa period because it corresponded to the longings of a whole people. Utamaro's work, dreamlike in its beauty, will therefore endure for ever.

Picture on the right: UTAMARO. From the series *Mother and Child*. The picture is irradiated by the brilliant green of the child's dress, around which all other tender tones, pink, yellow, light-brown, dark-brown, seem to be grouped. In this interesting composition everything is subordinated to one purpose alone—that of stressing the loveliness of the flowerlike child.
Signed: Utamaro hitsu. 36.5 × 23.5 cm.

Picture p. 106: UTAMARO. *Picture of a tiger*. With rough strokes of his brush, and using three tones of brown, Utamaro has painted this unusual animal picture. The bamboo stem and the leaves are shown black against a green background. The ground of the picture is yellowish.
Signed: Utamaro hitsu.
36 × 24 cm.

Picture p. 107: UTAMARO. *Yamauba with little Kintoki on her back combs her hair*.
Signed: Utamaro hitsu. 37.5 × 25.5 cm.

哥麿筆

近江屋

鴨

翡翠

二條羅法師

性　宿屋飯盛

小簑長依

Picture p. 108, above: UTAMARO. *Ducks and king-fisher*. On the left a poem, 1789, from: Ehon momo chidori; 100 plovers.
20 × 31 cm.

Picture p. 108, below: UTAMARO. From: *Ehon mushi erabi, A Selection of Insects,* 1788. Lotus leaf and duck-weed in a pool. On the right two poems. On the large leaf sits a brilliantly colored beetle, "koganemushi", "gold insect". The reflection in the water reveals to the green frog the little brown frog "kaeru" hiding under the broad leaf.
21 × 31 cm.

Color page: UTAMARO. *The Oiran Kasugano from the Tama-house with her Shinzo Uraba.* From: "Snow, Moon, Flowers compared to Women", representing the comparison with the flower. Beautiful Kasugano writes a love poem on the fan, admired by her Uraba, who stands by her side attired in a peach-red dress (the color of virginity). Signed: Utamaro hitsu. Publisher: Murataya.
38.5 × 25.5 cm.

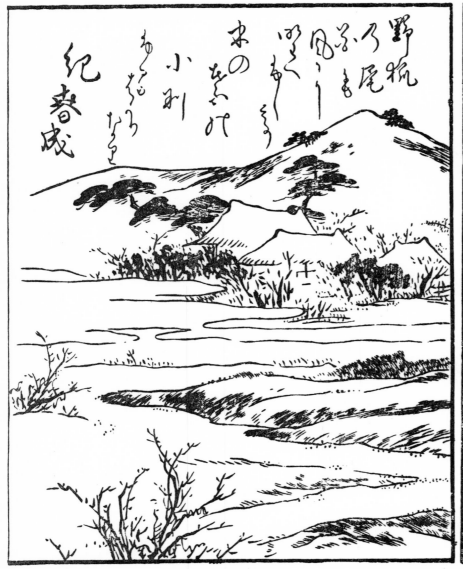

UTAMARO. *Landscape in the environment of Edo.* From
Ehon azuma asobi, 1790. 26.5 × 15.5 cm.

UTAMARO. *Lovers under an umbrella* from the series:
Furyu-ai-kio-kisoi. The lovers Djubei and Mori-
kawa. The woman in a white collar, pink undergarment and violet dress. The man in an undergarment striped pink and yellow. The umbrella is
grey on the outside, yellow on the inside.
Signed: Utamaro hitsu. Publishers: Kasendo.
36 × 23.5 cm.

Picture p. 112: UTAMARO. *A beauty from the Ogi-house sitting beside an elegant gentleman*, who wears the Mon of the Nakayama actors on his violet dress. Both smoke; he is putting down a sake bowl. She wears the butterfly headdress invented by the famous Hanaogi III, who belonged to the same Yoshiwara-house.

The ground of the picture is light-brown. The lady's undergarment is white, her dress pink, her Obi rust-red, her top garment black with yellow design.

Signed: Utamaro hitsu. Publisher: Tsuruya. 39 × 26 cm.

Preceding color page: EISHOSAI CHOKI, floruit 1772–1795. (The name "Choki" can also be read as Nagayoshi.) *Beauty from the Tozen-house in the shin-machi quarter of Osaka.*
Signed: Choki ga. Publisher: Tsutaya Yuzaburo. 38.5 × 25.8 cm.

Plate on p. 114: UTAMARO. Print of a line plate from the series Iitsu kioi iro no minakami. The picture represents the famed lovers, Miuraya Komurasaki and her bridegroom Shirai Gompachi, bidding farewell to one another at the entrance to the Yoshiwara-house. The line-block print reveals the beauty of Utamaro's drawing more clearly than the complete color print.
Signed: Utamaro hitsu. Publisher: Yohachi. 37.5 × 25.5 cm.

Picture p. 115: UTAMARO. A *young girl* with the sign of her house on her mallow-colored dress. Her Obi is green. The bright-red of her undergarment visible only at her wrist and her throat is repeated in the brilliant red of the smoking equipment lying on the windowsill near the fan.
Signed: Utamaro hitsu. 37.5 × 25.2 cm.

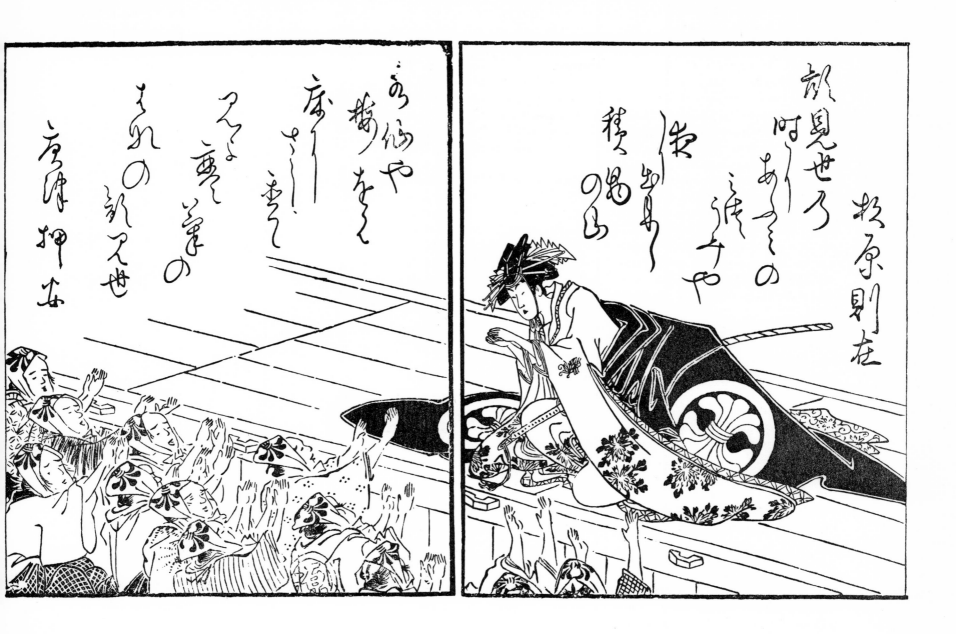

UTAMARO. *Segawa Kikunojo II, in a woman's part,*
acknowledges the applause from the stage. From the
book Ehon azuma asobi. March 1790.
26.5 × 15.5 cm.

Picture p. 116: UTAMARO. *Longings,* from a series
"Woman's Love". The dark-brown top garment,
the red undergarment and a sulphur-yellow comb
make the face appear white. The entire figure is
set on a pink mica ground, giving it an aristocratic
elegance.
Signed: Utamaro hitsu. Publishers: Tsutaya Jusaburo. 37 × 26 cm.

Spring 1794. The theatres of Edo are trying to stimulate the somewhat flagging interest of the public with the help of new actors' pictures. Edo's biggest publisher, Tsutaya Jusaburo, publishes them. They are large luxury prints on rich silver and mica grounds, used as a rule only for single sheet prints and *Surimono*. They bear the signature of an entirely unknown artist, Toshusai Sharaku. The splendor of these pictures creates a stir. They are bought eagerly by the theatre-goers, their success being such that the Government intervenes and prohibits this lavish treatment of theatre placards.

In May 1794 he had come to Tsutaya Jusaburo and offered his services. He represented himself as a No-player in the service of the Prince of Awa, giving his name as Saito Jurobei. In 50 days he drew the woodcuts for 23 large portraits of actors and 7 large double portraits—an extraordinary achievement. Few of these pictures appeared in a second edition. For Tsutaya Jusaburo the commission was a fiasco. If he himself had not had such confidence in their artistic quality, he would not have offered Sharaku more posters to draw, particularly in view of the fact that the Government had forbidden him to use the silver background in his pictures.

There then followed at longer intervals the small size actors' posters; it was only when these too failed to sell that Jusaburo abandoned the project and the artist retired.

Sharaku worked as a woodcut artist for some 300 days and during this period produced some 145 works which rank among the finest in the history of the Japanese woodcut.

His contemporaries refused him recognition as an artist. In the "Ukiyo-e ruiko", an Encyclopaedia of Artists appearing in 1798, it is stated:

"Sharaku lived in Edo Hacchobori.

Real name: ...

Pseudonym: Toshusai.

He drew actors' portraits but exaggerated reality and his pictures made a formless impression. Accordingly he had little success. After several years he gave up drawing..."

That is all his period has to say of an artist whom Europe justly considers one of the greatest in the Western sense.

Sharaku is a European discovery. As long ago as 1890 Bing counted him amongst the greatest, whereas neither the official Japanese history of the woodcut masters, published in 1900, nor the "Masterpieces of the Ukiyo-e School" 1905, contains a single reference to him.

European and American art dealers have made Sharaku's prints expensive and much sought after.

In the art of the Japanese woodcut Sharaku was neither a pioneer nor a reformer. He did not invent either the silver or mica grounds, which were in use long before his day. Shunko and Shunei were his models for the big, half length pictures, and Shunsho had been the first to introduce personal likeness into the actors' portraits. His great artistic achievement lies in the big portraits produced during the first few months of 1794.

Even though these pictures evoked no response in Japan, their significance for us is profound. No European work of art can rival their pathos. Far removed from realism as we understand it, these pictures reveal a realism of the soul which springs from entirely different sources.

These figures from the popular drama are eloquent of an enigmatic depth and a noble gravity and in their characterization rise to visionary heights.

To the European way of thinking and feeling Sharaku's mysterious life as an artist appears tragic. Such a belief is quite unfounded. The dates of his birth and death are not known.

It may be assumed that he returned to Awa in 1795 to engage once more in his original profession, for a list of No-players dated 1825 contains his name.

For us Westerners Sharaku's profound significance lies in the fact that his art is much nearer our own than is the classical Japanese art of his day, which with Kiyonaga had reached, and perhaps already passed, its zenith.

SHARAKU. *The actor Osagawa Tsuneyo II* as Masaoka Tsubone, a woman's part in the play Nihonmatsu Michinoku sodachi. Performed at the Kawarazaki-Theatre, Edo. Dress dark pink, top garment grey-green, undergarment white, collar with mica powder, dark mica ground.
Signed: Toshusai Sharaku ga. Publisher: Tsutaya Jusaburo. 36.5 × 24.8 cm.

SHARAKU. *The actor Nakayama Tomisaburo* as Echi-goya Umegawa and *the actor Ichikawa Komazo II* as Kameya Chubei in the drama Meido no Hikyaku. Dated July 20, 1794. The dresses of both are bluish, undergarments red, sashes black, umbrella yellow, umbrella-stick green, dark mica ground.
Signed: Toshusai Sharaku ga. Publisher: Jusa-buro. 37 × 25 cm.

Stage scene. Woodcut reproduction of a sketch in Chinese ink attributed to Sharaku.
Actual size.

SHARAKU. *The actor Ichikawa Ebizo IV* in the role of Kudo Suketsune, performed at the Kiri Theatre, Edo. Dress in the house-color of the Ichikawa, orange-brown, slate-colored cape, undergarments white, dark mica ground.
Signed: Toshusai Sharaku ga. Publisher: Tsutaya Jusaburo. 37.5 × 25 cm.

Silhouettes of actors backstage. Illustrations from an actor's book.
Actual size.

SHARAKU. *The actor Ichikawa Monnosuke II* in the part of Katanaya Hanshichi at the Kawarazaki Theatre. The dress is fawn, the undergarments bright-green and dark-red, the collar white, the ground silver.
Signed: Toshusai Sharaku ga. Publisher: Tsutaya Jusaburo. 37.8 × 25 cm.

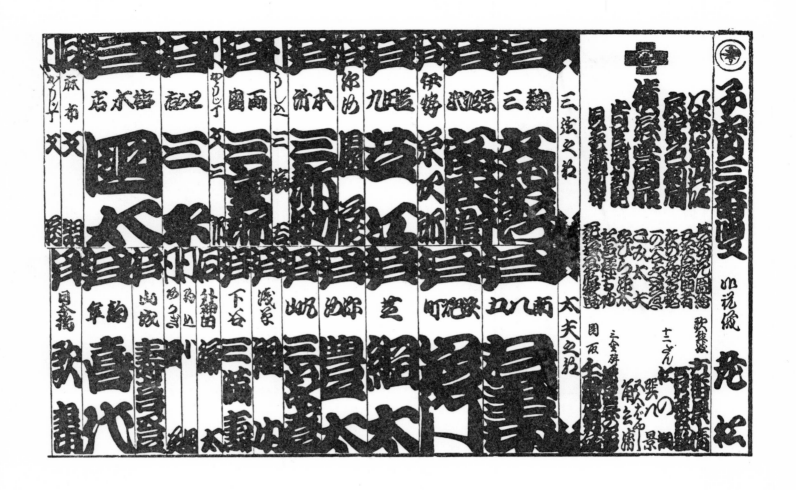

Detail of a theatre poster. 15×24 cm.

KABUKIDO ENKIO (floruit 1789–1800). *The actor Ichikawa Yaozo* performing the part of a Samurai in the play Sugawara Denju Tenarai Kagami at the Miyako Theatre, Edo, April 1796. Dress orange-brown, undergarment bright-red, face-paint red, toned mica ground.
Signed: Kabukido ga. 37×23 cm.

BUNRO about 1798. A minor master of the Utamaro period, independent of any school. Hayashi,
from whose collection this print comes, calls it
Young couple with two falcons.
The main attraction of the picture is its color composition, which vies with the best Utamaro.
Signed: Bunro ga. 33 × 21.5 cm.

The elder of the two sons of Gorobei the wood-carver was called Kumakichi, the "Lucky Bear". The wood-carver's workshop, where small actors' figures had been produced en masse since the sweeping success of father Gorobei's Danjuro statuettes, must have been the world of little "Lucky Bear". The workshop, situated near the Shiba-Shimmei Temple in Mishima Street, was held in high esteem, and it is understandable that Kumakichi and his brother, who was five years his junior, should have first tried their hand at wood-carving.

At the age of 14, however, we find the boy apprenticed to Utagawa Toyoharu, who, in 1785, bestowed upon him the title of Utagawa Toyokuni. He adopted one style after the other; now we recognize in his pictures the influence of Shunsho's "Beauties from the Green Houses", and then occasionally meet with a Shunman figure. Or we find him imitating the *Uki*, landscapes with a perspective by his teacher, so that sometimes the signature is the only clue to the painter's identity. He imitated the artistic idiom of Utamaro and of Kiyonaga, even that of his own disciple Kunisada. All his life Toyokuni was on the look-out for artists with something to teach him. He was too modest to believe in himself, though he succeeded in producing some wonderful compositions, e.g. the *Ehon Imago Sugata*, published about 1802, a work on women in two volumes, with a postscript written by himself. He reached the height of his creative activity about 1803, when he produced his actor portraits and his triptychs.

According to the carved inscription on his tombstone his amiable personality won him many pupils, including some from the "Red Gate", i.e. the Imperial Palace. Other noble disciples, such as Prince Hifuga of Kameyama Castle, who granted

UTAGAWA TOYOKUNI
(1769–1825)

TOYOKUNI I. Chinese ink sketch for an actor's portrait. Actual size.

TOYOKUNI I. *The actor Bando Mitsugoro* in the role of the merchant Jubei. This, probably Toyokuni's best actor portrait, is printed in two colors only, grey and bright-red. The fan and the cuff, where the undergarment becomes visible, are bright-red. The collar, the ground of which is bright-red, is printed over with black. The sash is treated in the same way; patches are in relief pressing.
Signed: Toyokuni ga. Publisher: Tsuruya.
39×25.8 cm.

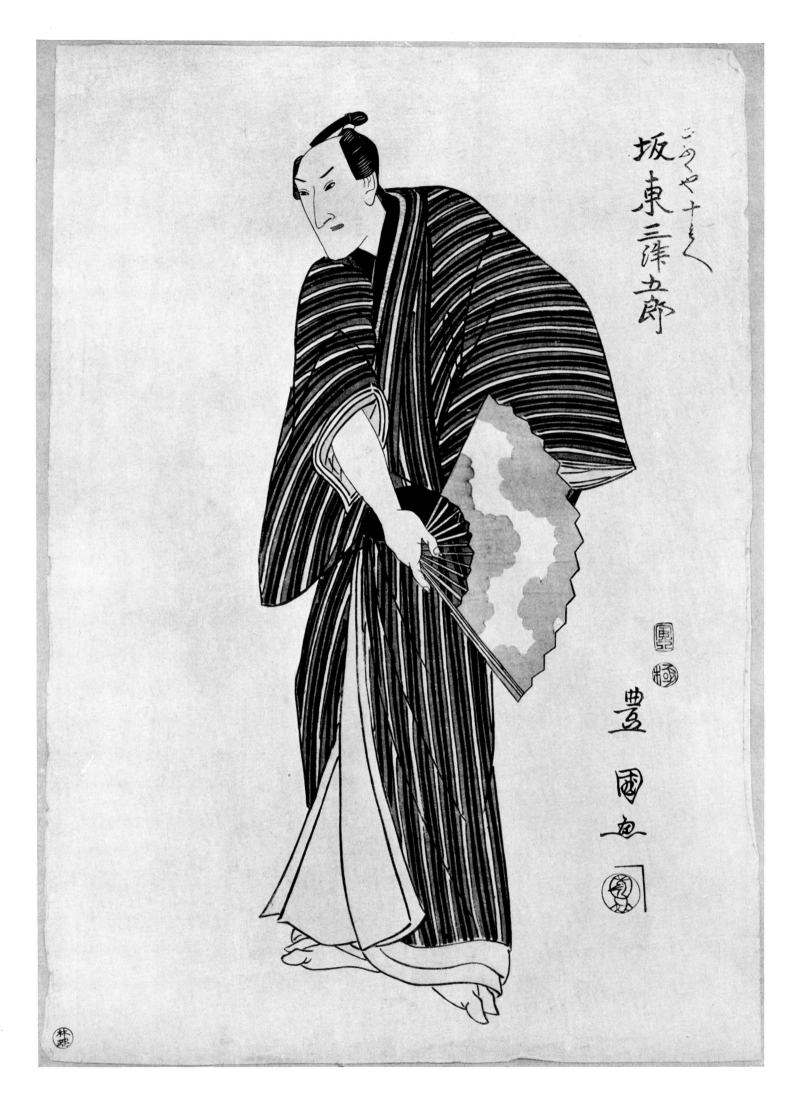

坂東三津五郎

豊国画

131

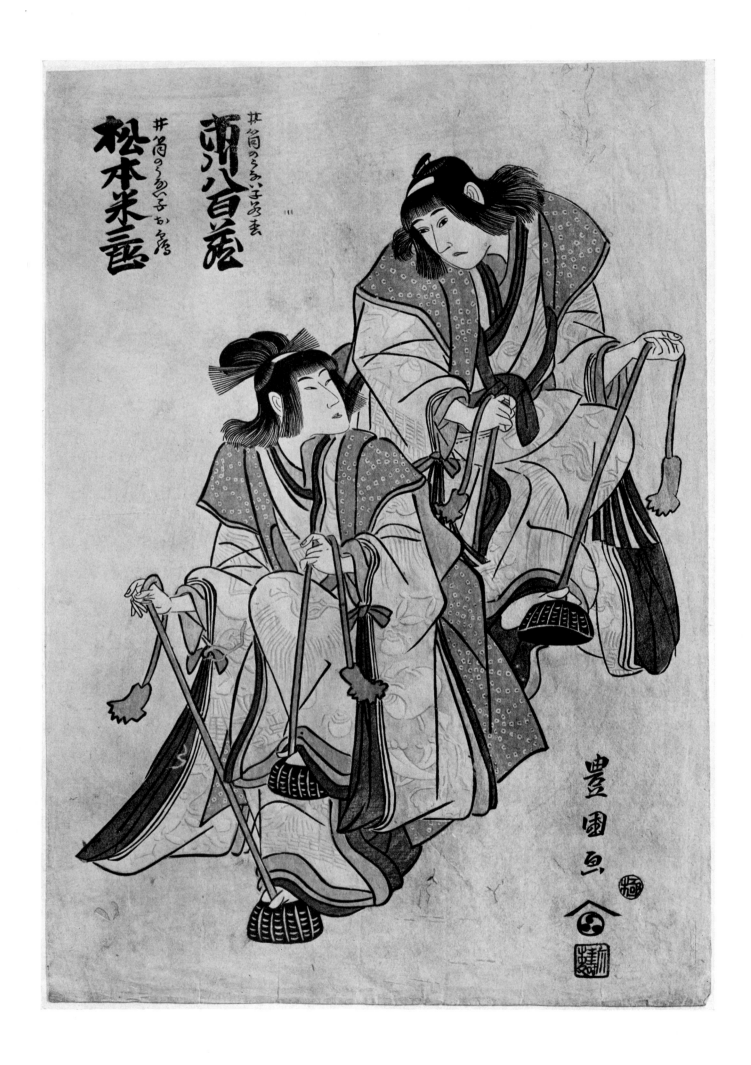

Double spread pages: TOYOKUNI I. *A Princess and her suite on a walk*. Pentaptych. Fuji, standing out against the grey background, towers white above the blue-green forests. The dominant colors of the dresses are violet with blue, or ochre-yellow with grey. Each color appears in several variations, each print has its own color accent, and the five prints together form an interesting color rhythm.
Signed: Toyokuni ga. Publisher: Wakasaya Yoichi, Edo. 5 × 39.5 × 25 cm.

Picture p. 134: TOYOKUNI. *Two actors in parts from a Joruri play*. Ichikawa-Yaozo as a boy and Matsumoto Yonesaburo as a girl playing with stilts. A carefully executed theatre poster. Dress pattern in blind-pressing, the raised parts white, the sunken parts yellow. Upper garments grey.
Signed: Toyokuni ga. Publisher: Eijudo. 37 × 25 cm.

him the right to use the *Toshi dama*, the ring-stamp as his crest, enhanced his glory. As a teacher Toyokuni was unsurpassed. His Utagawa school was the biggest and most ramified of all the artists' clans that ever existed in Japan. It produced great masters, such as Kunisada and Kuniyoshi, but even these belong to the period of decadence, when the art of the woodcut was in its decline.
The Utagawa clan followed an original custom in naming an artist. The founder, for instance, gave his pupils the first syllable of his name to form the first syllable of theirs: Toyoharu—Toyokuni, Toyohiro.
The pupils of Toyoharu, in their turn, gave their pupils the second syllable of their names: Toyohiro—Hiroshige, Hirokage, etc.; Toyokuni—Kunisada, Kuniyoshi, etc. All "Kuni" are the pupils of Toyokuni.
The next generation of pupils received the ultimate syllable of their teachers' names: Kunisada—Sadatora, Sadakage, Sadahiro, etc.; Kuniyoshi—Yoshihide, Yoshitoshi, Yoshimaru, etc.
A certain confusion was caused in this system by the death of Toyokuni I, henceforth the name of Toyokuni being used not only by his pupil Kunishige, but, wrongly, by the very prolific Kunisada as well.
To what extent Toyokuni was able to influence his pupils, despite the great number attending his school, we cannot say. It is certain that even in age he was esteemed. He died on February 24, 1825, aged 57, and was buried in the Koun-zen Temple. At Yanagishima his pupils erected a memorial stone to him on which they had carved the whole life story of their teacher, "whose name rose like the sun".

KEISAI EISEN
(1790–1848)

Color print: KEISAI EISEN (1790–1848). *Carp jumping the waterfall*.
Signed: Keisai hitsu. Stamp: Eisen. 71.5 × 24.7 cm.

The artist Eisen was a titanic figure, as intense in his enjoyment as in his work. An orphan from the age of 14, he earned his livelihood and supported his younger brothers and sisters by writing poems. He became a famous Haikai poet and, later, a dramatic critic. As a sideline he studied painting under the Kano masters and, subsequently, under Kuniyoshi; and finally, after returning from his wanderings, joined Hokusai and Hiroshige. His work includes wonderful landscapes, *Surimonos* and feminine portraits, all of them original and vigorous. The Carp in the Waterfall was one of the most famous woodcuts of its time.
In 1843 he wrote to a friend that he was about to give up painting, "I prefer to laugh at the art of others rather than have them laugh at mine". He died in 1848 at Edo, aged nearly 59.

Color page on the right: KEISAI EISEN. Eisen's forceful personality is revealed in the powerful lines and surfaces with which he portrays this beauty. The name of the whole series is: *Present Day Beauty Contest*. In the small, round mirror is written "little courtesan".
Signed: Keisai Eisen. Publisher: Sanoki.
37.5 × 25.8 cm.

Picture p. 137: KUNISADA. Actor in the role of Daiku Rokubei (Carpenter Rokubei) from the series: Famous dramas.
Signed: Gototei Kunisada, gwa; many-colored on glimmer ground; 245 × 255.

UOYA HOKKEI
(1780–1850)
(vide p. 164 und 166)

Illustration from Fujin Gazoshu. *Japanese poetesses*. 1806. 18 × 12.8 cm.

Katsushika Hokusai, the best known of the Japanese woodcut masters in Europe and the most popular among the Japanese people, was born in 1760 in Honjo, a suburb of Edo, in the Katsushika district. There, among the ramshackle workshops of the artisans and traders, he lived and died, a son of the people, to whom he was passionately devoted, and whom his art immortalised. There, one of the most popular poets of his time, he wrote novels and poems; there he painted his pictures, 35,000 of which have been preserved for posterity. The achievements of this fanatical worker are of gigantic dimensions; their execution must surely have taxed the limits of physical endurance.

Hokusai was the adopted child of an artisan, a mirror-grinder. Tokitaro, as he was called as a child, spent his early days in an environment of craftsmen, where diligence and manual labor formed the very basis of existence and were esteemed above everything else. In his father's workshop the boy must have pressed his nose against the cool surfaces of the metal mirrors, which reflected so mysteriously the skilfully represented objects on the back; and he may there have had his first inklings of a world beyond reality, the realm of art. At the end of the 19th century European biographers, conforming to the fashion of the day, went to all possible lengths—and beyond—to glorify his origins by elevating his father to the rank of Imperial mirror-maker, and making his mother the illegitimate daughter of the Kira, and thus a born princess. Whether Hokusai's father Nakajima Ise actually supplied the Court with mirrors or not seems wholly irrelevant today. That his mother might have been the daughter of the Kira assassinated in December 1702 is definitely ruled out by Hokusai's birthdate, 1760. His mother's maiden name was Hehachiro, indicating her descent from a family which had once been the victim of a blood-feud of the Forty-Seven Ronin. Hokusai repeatedly mentioned this fact, and he may well have inherited from his mother his unyielding pride, which he preserved through all his misery. Yet the world into which Hokusai was born was and remained definitely that of the suburban people of Honjo. The first faces which little Tokitaro beheld bent over his cradle were the good-natured, wrinkled faces of the neighbors: pedlars, traders, vagrants and story-tellers of the street. They entertained the boy with their imitations of fabled figures; they taught him fairy stories and ancient folksongs. The mature artist's enchanting pictures are nothing but the vision of his childhood, evoking all the simplicity and vitality of his first experiences.

He cast off the shackles of his environment at an early age. His brothers freed him from his obligation to follow in his father's steps, thus we find him at the age of ten as errand boy in a bookshop. It is here that, according to his own statement, he made up his mind to become a draftsman. Just then Japan's production of illustrated books, tales of love and chivalry and horror stories, had reached its height. It is easy to imagine the deep impression made by such reading upon the boy's receptive mind. Young Hokusai amidst piles of books deeply engrossed in a book of woodcuts is a favourite subject of Japanese illustrations. But dreaming was not Tokitaro's lot. He had to work, and to work with his hands; to become an artisan like his father. Thus he chose wood-carving as his trade, becoming at 13 an apprentice in a wood-carving studio in Yokoami, a neighborhood in the Henjo district in which he lived as well as worked. This was the second of the 92 dwellings which the eternal wanderer was to occupy during his life. He now styled himself Tetsuzo, the first of his 50 odd fancy names. In the Yokoami studio he learnt the art of wood-engraving, an art which he utilized later with such consummate skill in his painting. For here in the wood-engraver's studio a great variety of drawings and color-tone pictures passed through his hands daily. Not only were the apprentices trained in the use of the engraving implements but also how to adapt themselves to the styles of various artists, and to cut their plates so as to reproduce in print an absolutely exact copy of the brushwork. Such virtuosity could only be attained by the round-about way of copying with the brush. When a drawing or a color-tone sketch was delivered at the studio for engraving, the apprentices began by preparing one or two copies with the brush, in order to keep a reference copy should the engraving fail, for the original drawing had to be pasted on the woodblock and was thus destroyed in the engraving process. There exist numerous pictures which Hokusai signed as wood-engraver, e.g. the illustrations to a novel by Sancho printed in 1775. This also proves how gifted the boy was—for he would not otherwise have been entrusted with the preparation of

HOKUSAI. Shika Sashinkio, *Portraits of Poets*, 1830. Leaning against the balustrade of a roof terrace, high above the sea, a Chinese dignitary contemplates the moon. It is the Japanese poet Nakamaro, who set out to see the world and became a Minister of the Emperor of China. Nakamaro once wrote a poem: "When his soul wanders across the skies, and encounters the silvery moon, the moon that once shone upon him in his youth in the mountains of Mikaza near Kasuga, then he remembers his home country Japan, and finds solace for the tribulations of life." The poem brought Nakamaro into disfavour, and he returned to Japan.

The vermilion of the strangely shaped rock in the foreground shines out against the deep-blue of the sea and the green of the tree.

Signed: Zen Hokusai Iitsu hitsu. Publisher: Moriya Jihei. 50.2 × 22 cm.

blocks after only a year's apprenticeship. Hokusai himself indicates the year 1775 as the beginning of his artistic activity; it was when he produced his first drawings, which were printed later. It must have been about this time that he wrote his first poems, and approximately a year later his first novel. Hokusai says in a note: "Until the age of 19 (his 18th year according to our way of counting, as the Japanese add one pre-natal year to their age) I was a wood-engraver, then I gave up this profession and became a painter." This happened when he joined Shunsho's studio. Shunsho, the most famous master of actor portraits, was then at the height of his career, and Hokusai's colleagues in his studio, Shunko, Shunman, Shunei, and Shunsen, were the foremost masters of the classical woodcut. All called themselves Katsukawa, and the first syllable in their otherwise arbitrarily formed names was that of their master.

In their illustrious company Hokusai's artistic ambition was aroused. Very soon he received the master-title of a Katsukawa and from then on called himself Katsu-

HOKUSAI. *Surimono with a New Year's poem by Hokusai*. In the New Year season, the poem runs, the young and charming girls from the provinces flock to the Imperial City to sell their wood and flowers. A kite flown by children has come to rest on the bundle of wood. The muted tones of the red and green pattern blend with the olive-green of dress and kerchief.
Signed: Hokusai ga. 21.4 × 18.4 cm.

HOKUSAI. Original drawing for the wood-cut-block maker (Chinese ink painting on silk paper) as full page illustration for a book "History of the Isle Hachi-jo". A man in the attitude of resolution and a weeping woman on a moonlit house terrace. 18.5 × 13.7 cm.

kawa Shunro. Apart from actor portraits in the Shunsho style Shunro also published, from 1781 on, book illustrations. Poetry was his sideline. He wrote novels and Haikai verse which brought him popularity; he studied the old masters of the Kano and Tosa schools, and decorated fans and various *objets d'art* with his painting. Hokusai's odd incognito existence, with its permanent change of residence and name, considerably complicated the work of his later biographers. He was an ascetic, drank neither tea nor wine and lived only for his art. During his eight years at Shunsho's studio he also produced the cheap, short novels known, because of their yellow cover, as Kibyoshi, which he wrote and illustrated himself. In the novel "With a polite word everything is permitted" he names himself as poet Korewassai, as painter Shunro; in 1782 he published the novel *Kamakura* under the pen-name "Gummatei". The whole period of his activity at the Shunsho studio was dominated by a fanatical quest for the ultimate artistic verities, an attitude which frequently placed him at loggerheads with his master and his school. For side by side with his wood engraving work he indulged in brush painting and in studying the old masters. The increased consciousness of his own worth was accompanied by a growing estrangement from his school, and in the prevailing atmosphere of mutual irritation the slightest incident could cause a final break. Once, when Katsukawa Shunko, a colleague of Hokusai, discovered a Hokusai poster in the Kano style outside the shop of an art dealer, he considered it an outrage to the honour of the Katsukawa, and angrily tore it to pieces. This was the end of Hokusai's Katsukawa period. He renounced his Katsukawa name, went his own way, and took the most important step of his artistic career by finally breaking his links with school and tradition.

His way to independence and greatness led through hunger and poverty. He moved from studio to studio, learning with amazing speed, but never satisfied with his own achievements and never staying for long. It is interesting to note that Hokusai's education during this period chiefly followed the lines of the academic, classical school, at certain times abandoning the Ukiyo altogether. When his earnings ceased he took to peddling in order to keep his family alive, selling, among his other wares, his own Kibyoshi, which he drew, engraved and printed himself. Once, when selling red pepper in the marketplace, he noticed his master Shunsho approaching. He was so ashamed that he left his baskets and hid in the crowd. Yet Hokusai could not live without his art. As soon as he earned a gold piece for painting a May flag he rushed back into artistic activity. This increased from year to year and led him, this time, to success. Nevertheless, he remained poor to the very end. Living only for his art and scorning money and fame, he would hardly have known how to keep money even if fortune had smiled upon him.

His poverty has often led to the erroneous assumption that he must have been esteemed little in his time, though the well-known *Makimono* story, related by Edmond de Goncourt in his "Hokusai" (1896), proves the contrary. Once a Dutchman named Isbert Hemmel commissioned two *Makimono;* one represented the life of the Japanese man, the other that of the Japanese woman. The price for the two was fixed at 150 *Ryo.* (In 1818 1 *Ryo* was equivalent to 2 Nishuban gold dollars.) The ship's doctor, who had come to Edo with Hemmel, commissioned two copies of the two pictures from Hokusai and also offered a fee of 150 *Ryo.* When Hokusai arrived to deliver his pictures, the doctor raised various objections and offered him only half the agreed amount. Hokusai rejected the offer, and when the doctor declared himself willing to purchase one of the two pictures for 75 *Ryo,* Hokusai rolled up both of them and went home. His wife was horrified, having already pledged even these 75 *Ryo* for old debts. Hokusai's pride, however, was outraged at the fact that a stranger should break his word, and he is reported to have remarked afterwards to Hemmel: "Better suffer misery than degradation." Hemmel paid the 150 *Ryo* and also purchased the copies.

Hokusai painted his first *Surimono* in 1793, thus opening a particularly happy phase in his artistic career. The *Surimono*, in use since the middle of the 18th century, is an elaborately artistic congratulation, an invitation to a concert, to a festivity, or a New Year's greeting. Wealthy Japanese use it to convey their compliments and invitations to a select circle of friends. In this kind of art Hokusai was unexcelled. Inexhaustible in his inspiration, his inherent decorative gift enabled him, through his superb technique, to elaborate the simplest theme to a most sumptuous pictorial effect.

HOKUSAI. Shokoku Takimeguri, journey to the famous waterfalls, 1827. *The Ono Fall on the Kiso road.*
Signed: Zen Hokusai Iitsu hitsu. Publisher: Eijudo 37.5 × 25.5 cm.

HOKUSAI. Page from Shimpen Suiko Gaden, *New translation of the Suiko-Den*.
One of the 108 heroes of this story of noble robbers, so popular in China. The hero is Gunsun-Scheng, called Ju-yün-lung, "the Dragon that enters the Clouds".
Publisher: Marukaya, 1807. 18.5 × 25.5 cm.

147

やのどをくらつるふ
すどなー
やのどをひきつるか
そのど
よとふくあり

天下一のものゝんともあるべき

のぐをやとい

It may be of some interest to quote the text of the first *Surimono* ordered by a musician, as it gives a glimpse of the social life of the period:

"In the hope that you enjoy the best of health, despite the oppressive heat, I beg to inform you that in view of my great public success I have changed my name, and that, to inaugurate with due solemnity my new name, I am arranging on the fourth day of the coming month a concert at the home of Kioya in Riogoku from ten o'clock in the morning until four o'clock in the afternoon, with the participation of all my pupils. The performance will take place irrespective of the weather. I count on the honour of your presence. Tokiwazu Mozitayu."

The picture portrayed a young merchant surrounded by the various utensils of his trade. It shows that the *Surimono* picture was not necessarily an illustration of the festivity to which it referred, though at a later date the Uta-poets and the painters harmonized the poem and picture with the occasion of the *Surimono*.

Hundreds of *Surimonos* were produced (see p. 144), and Hokusai's fame as master of this particular form of graphic art was soon established beyond challenge. His pupils Hokkei and Gakutei devoted themselves exclusively to the *Surimono* and their great mastery preserved Hokusai's glory for decades.

At the end of the century we find Hokusai, now forty years of age, collaborating with other leading artists, such as Utamaro, in a common task. The magnificent

HOKUSAI. A page from Gado Hitori Keiko, *Drawing Self Taught*, 1815. A humorous drawing demonstrating that the syllable character of the word Kagamiya (mirror grinder) can be transformed into the picture of a mirror grinder.
15.2 × 11.2 cm.

HOKUSAI. Still life in various tones of blue, in the manner of Delft porcelain painting.
Signed: Zen Hokusai hitsu. Stamp. Publisher: Moriya Jihei. Actual size.

148

149

colored albums of the *Yehon azuma-asobi*, the *Toto shokei ichiran*, and the *Sumidagawa riogan* were produced; all portray the environments of Edo, gradually bringing the landscape to the fore at the expense of the figures. Shiba Kokan initiated Hokusai in the technique of European perspective, and Hokusai succeeded magnificently in blending Eastern and Western forms of pictorial structure to create something new of his own. Thus the Hokusai landscape, which 20 years later found its ultimate and perfect expression in the 36 Fuji pictures, was born. To Hokusai nothing now appeared beyond his reach. He searched for a new painting technique—instead of his brush he painted with his fingers, with a bottle, with an egg, with his left hand, from the bottom upwards, from left to right. Success crowned all his efforts. Months on end these experiments robbed him of sleep, for he was convinced that his virtuosity, his supreme technical accomplishments were an obstacle to true art. He wrote books about painting, wishing to leave to his pupils his artistic testa-

HOKUSAI. At the frontier between Etchu and Hida the precarious rope bridge hangs high above reddish clouds, forests and peaks. A blue mountain range emerges from light clouds, and a flight of birds enhances the depth of space surrounding the bridge in the skies.
The Tsuri-hashi, *the Hanging Bridge*, belongs to the series "Journey to the Famous Bridges", produced between 1827 and 1830.
Signed: Zen Hokusai Iitsu hitsu. Publisher: Eijudo. 25.5 × 38 cm.

HOKUSAI. Original drawing for the woodcut engraver (Chinese ink on silk paper). Half-page illustration to the book "History of the Isle Hachi-jo, 1816". The hero sets foot on the island, Evil flees. 18.5 × 13.7 cm.

ment. "Never use the color before it has come to rest; and before removing the dirt from the surface of the water, the color must be stirred with the finger, never with the brush"; or, "There is antique black and fresh black, lustrous black and mat black, a light black and a dark black. Antique black must be mixed with red, whereas fresh black tolerates only blue", etc. Such are the recipes we find in the books of the period.

Despite his success Hokusai remained modest, plucking up his courage after periods of great need to search again for artistic perfection, the ultimate aim of his passionate quest. How moving are the last words which the dying Hokusai, aged 90, addressed to his daughter, who nursed him: "If heaven would grant me ten more years, or even only five, I might still become a great artist". In paying much attention to the landscape in his pictures Hokusai followed the trend of his time. Japan had experienced an awakening of interest in the countryside; people traveled, admired nature, and a flourishing literature offered the illustrators an opportunity to meet the new demand. In Hokusai's pictures centre and background are still reminiscent of stage backdrops, and strange horizontal cloud strips, as found in old Chinese pictures, obtrude into the foreground. However, his works freed themselves increasingly from tradition and school. The trees and hedges, given characters of their own, stand there as individual objects. The horizons recede, and his pictures have "atmosphere". Whereas the landscape was once only framework, mere trimming to the human figure, it is now man who serves as trimming to the magnificent scene. Where man alone is represented, however, he is no longer rigid, his hidden forces seem freed, and the picture pulsates with the warm breath of life. At the close of the century, Hokusai's literary and artistic works testify to the fermentation and change in the artist's soul.

This state of mind is also revealed in his original attempt to confound his enemies, who called him "the painter of little pictures", by producing a colossal painting "on a scale that the world has not yet seen". It was in Edo, near the Gokokdji Temple, about 1804, that he painted one such gigantic picture on paper. Later, for similar reasons, he painted in Nagoya an even larger picture. The performance has been described by Hokusai's friend Yenko-an as follows:

"In the centre of the Northern court, protected by a fence, a specially manufactured sheet of paper, many times as thick as our raincoats, was unfolded. The size of the paper was 120 mats (194 square meters). To keep it taut the ground was covered with a thick layer of rice-straw and wooden blocks were placed on it as weights at short distances to prevent the wind from blowing the paper away. A scaffolding was mounted on the temple wall, provided with pulleys and long ropes by which the picture could be hoisted. The top end of the paper was fastened to a huge oak beam, to which the ropes were attached. Brushes had been provided, the smallest of which was the size of a broom. The ink had been prepared in large tubs, and now stood ready in barrels. The preparations lasted the whole morning. People crowded the court from the early hours—noblemen and peasants, women and girls, old men and children. At noon Hokusai, accompanied by his pupils, appeared attired in a strange, semi-ceremonial dress, his legs and arms bare. The pupils filled bronze vats with paint, carrying them behind the master while he worked. First Hokusai took a brush the size of a bunch of hay, dipped it in a vat of paint, and drew with it the right and then the left eye of the Daruma. After that he ran several steps and painted the mouth and ear. Thereafter came the neck, the hair, the beard. With another brush, which he dipped in lighter paint, he drew other lines. His pupils then carried along a gigantic vat containing a brush of rice-sacks bundled together, and dripping with Chinese ink. When they had placed the brush on the spot Hokusai indicated, the artist tied a rope around his neck and around the brush and, running backwards with little steps and dragging the brush, drew the outlines of Daruma's dress. The red surfaces were colored with paint spooned out with a ladle from buckets. To prevent it from running several pupils followed behind mopping it up with damp cloths. By nightfall the gigantic Daruma picture was ready and was hoisted by rope and the pulley, in passing touching the crowd who milled round it in a buzz of excitement like ants round a piece of cake which has fallen onto an anthill."

This feat had, as a contemporary document put it, the effect of a "thunderbolt". Hokusai became popular overnight, and the people's acclamation caused him greater happiness than honours and recognition bestowed upon him from higher

HOKUSAI. *Kohada Koheji appears before his murderer at the burning mosquito net*. Taken from: "100 Stories, 1830."
Not signed. 25 × 18.5 cm.

HOKUSAI. *The Ship-bridge over the Tonegawa, in Sano, Kosuka Province* is the name Hokusai gives this picture, part of the series "Journey to the Famous Bridges". The deep-blue of the river is enhanced by the landscape covered with freshly fallen snow.
Signed: Zen Hokusai Iitsu hitsu. Publisher: Eijudo.
25.2 × 36.8 cm.

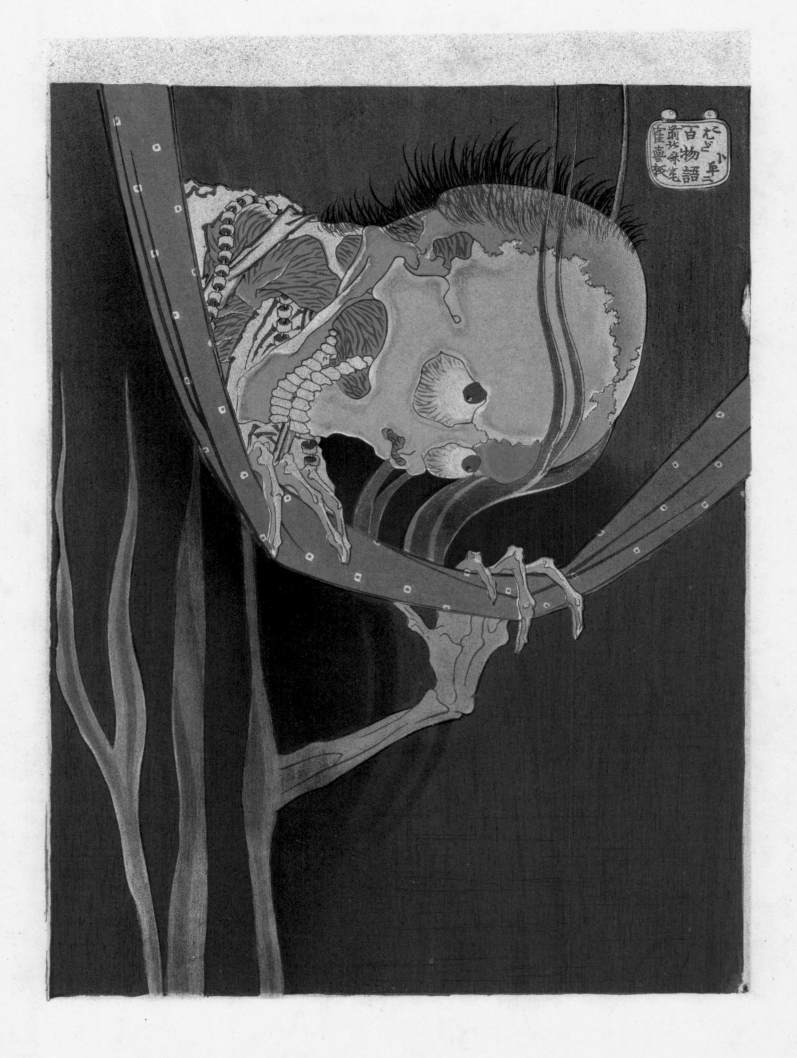

153

154

quarters. For his beloved Honjo he painted a gigantic horse of similar proportions, and soon his fame reached the Imperial Court. Returning from hawking the Shogun desired to see this people's idol, and Hokusai was ordered to appear in the Dempo Temple to show him "the new art". The chronicles vary in their descriptions of the meeting; wherein they agree, and what may be assumed as certain, can be described as follows: Hokusai lifted a paper door of the temple from its hinges, and placed it on the floor of the hall. Taking indigo paint with his hands from a container he threw it on the paper, then brushed it with his hand. He then took a cock from a basket he had brought with him, daubed its claws with red stamp dye, and let it run over the paper. Bowing deeply to the Shogun, he is reported to have called out: "This is the Tatsuta". But all those present had already recognized the blue Tatsuta, the river of the poets, with the red maple leaves floating on it. The Shogun Ieharu was pleased, and Hokusai was wildly fêted. This episode reveals two important aspects: firstly, Hokusai was granted the highest honour ever

HOKUSAI. The sacred mountain towers above blue waters and clouds. The two fishermen silhouetted on the shore combine with the outlines of the rock and fishing-lines to make a design which repeats the contours of Fujiyama. Waves and breakers moving in the opposite direction form, together with the pyramid of Fuji, the Chinese character for mountain. The print is part of a series of 36 Fuji pictures produced between 1823 and 1829.
Signed: Zen Hokusai Iitsu hitsu. Publisher: Eijudo, Edo. 25.8 × 37.7 cm.

HOKUSAI. A page from Ehon tekinurai, a correspondence course in education. The book, containing over 200 illustrations, represents such a rich source of information on life in old Japan that for fifty years the Government would not permit it to be sent abroad.
The magnificent writing is that of the 14th century, parallel to it runs the Kana, the explanatory script. Edition 1828. 18 × 12.5 cm.

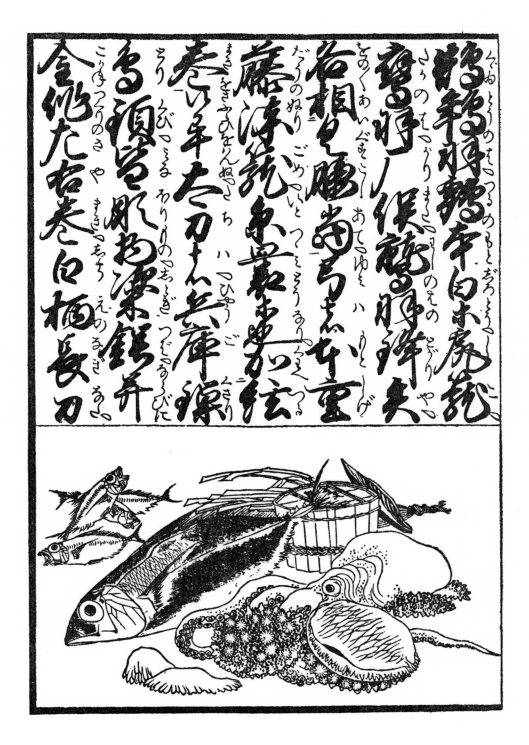

bestowed upon an artist in his day. In the second place, the incident proves Hokusai's unerring artistic intuition, for it was not his intention to demonstrate his superior craftsmanship, but to indicate that virtuosity and technical accomplishment have nothing to do with art.

The people's jubilation was boundless. It is said that Hokusai's residence was beleaguered by the masses for months on end. Everyone desired a signed drawing or at least an autograph, or some other souvenir from the master. The artists, too, began to seek his counsel and inspiration. But Hokusai rapidly retired again into his incognito existence and worked obsessed, forgetful of honour and success.

We are now entering the period in which he published, jointly with Bakin, in 1807 the Spirit-Book of the Kasane in six volumes.

Collecting impressions and sketching them, he endeavoured to master the visions of the world and of the spirit that beset him. His ghost pictures record with cruel force the most horrifying images ever to emanate from the brain of man.

After a collaboration of five years, Edo's two most popular artists, the poet Bakin and the painter Hokusai, separated for good, and Hokusai turned to free drawing. *Mangwa*, the first volume of which appeared in 1814, is a collection of sketches, frequently of a touching naïveté, with a thousand irrelevant drawings and sudden flashes of inspired art. Between 1814 and 1849 fifteen of these volumes full of impressions of the moment appeared. Volume 14 (1875) and volume 15 (1878) were printed after his death.

Immediately upon the publication of the first *Mangwa* volume a number of important artists formed a group round Hokusai, who endeavoured to instruct them in his principles by means of books and model sketches, among them the *Shashin Gafu* published about 1814. Of all the text books for the teaching of drawing produced by Hokusai, the *Shashin Gafu*—literally, an album of nature-copies—is the most important. In it Hokusai demonstrates for the first time his own new style, which makes *tabula rasa* with tradition and school. Nor did he leave it at the *Shashin Gafu*. Similar publications followed each other in quick succession—*Hokusai Soga*, "Rough Drawings", *Denshin Gwakio*, "Mirror of Drawings", and many more. In the *Kwacho Gaden* Hokusai collected all his animal and plant studies. There we find the fairy bird Otori hovering above a seascape, the descent of the wild geese into the reeds enhancing the great decorative effect of the composition. With the 36 Fuji pictures a new plane is reached. Produced between 1823 and 1829, their success was such that Hokusai increased their number to 46. He was now entering the last phase of his maturity. Entirely free from the grip of convention and school, the master, now at the apogee of his art, formed his pictures with supreme self-assurance. It is not by chance that he chooses the Fuji as his theme; to every Japanese the sacred mountain is the symbol of all that is exalted and beautiful. Hokusai's Fuji series remains unexcelled; and posterity is justified in regarding them as works of the highest artistic quality.

If the Japanese masters placed man as a complex linear composition in the foreground, grouping the landscape around him, Hokusai, on the contrary, fits man as part of nature into the harmonious linear structure of the landscape; in several of his Fuji pictures he omits the human element altogether.

A picture like the Fuji on a bright day, for instance, is a single luminous chromatic harmony of a sonority and depth never hitherto achieved by a Western artist. The pictorial composition of the Fuji landscapes is totally new, radically different from anything the artistic world had been used to. Let us consider the landscape near Hodogaya (p. 158). Here Hokusai does not endeavour to grasp the forest as a whole by subordinating the individual to the general; on the contrary, from the single phenomena, the tree-tops, he creates the whole—the wood. Hokusai's pictures, like a movement in music, are composed of variations on a motif. A character, the motif, is borrowed from Chinese writing. It is repeated in the horseman, and in the sedan-chair carriers, who are also variations of the same character, the character for mountain. Hokusai's pictures are therefore not copied from reality, but are consciously constructed works, as genuine and alive in their rhythm as nature itself.

Despite his entire independence of all older schools, Hokusai frequently resorted, and with profounder understanding than any other painter of his time, to the formal tradition of the classical Sino-Japanese art. He used its symbolism extensively; and this not merely conventionally, but from his own immediate inward experience. His most famous picture "The Fuji seen from Kanagawa", usually

HOKUSAI. The black-and-white reproduction cannot do justice to the dreamlike, blue serenity of the colored picture. Apart from the grey tones of Fuji all the other colors are variations of sky-blue. The mysterious parallelism of the lines indicates the quest for a symbolic form. Even the reflection of Fuji in the water had to undergo an unnatural displacement to fit into the symbol pattern. The picture is called *Fuji mirrors itself in the water*. The quiet little village is Mizako, in Koshu Province. Signed: Zen Hokusai Iitsu hitsu. Publisher: Eijudo, Edo. 25.3 × 37 cm.

157

158

referred to as "Hokusai's Wave", demonstrates this best. Here he separates sky and water by a line, giving the two parts of the picture a definite similarity to the two interlocking vortices of the Yin-Yang sign, which symbolizes the interplay of the active and passive forces in the universe, the white summit of the Fujiyama in the dark sky being substituted for the white pole in the dark field of the sign.

Such symbolic forms, which may evoke a variety of associations in the Eastern observer, must not be conceived as elements extraneous to the picture, or artificially tacked on to it. The extraordinarily powerful impression created by this well-known work, with the written characters it incorporates, proves that such a form of composition is justified. The sensual expression of a depicted phenomenon—for instance that of rising and subsiding waves—becomes itself symbolic if reduced to its essential features, and therefore quite naturally coincides with the suggestive traditional symbol. Only a master of Hokusai's stature could visualise the ultimate correspondence between the definite significance of a geometrical figure and the suggestive delineations of a sensual reality.

Simultaneously with and after the Fuji pictures Hokusai published a series of books and single sheet prints, The Waterfalls, 1827 to 1830, and the magnificent *Ehon Teikin-Orai*, an old textbook on education, which he revived by painting the text with the wonderful characters of the 14th century, and illustrating it with 200 scenes from the life of the people.

At 68, shortly after the publication of the *Teikin-Orai*, Hokusai had a stroke. But his iron will triumphed over this blow, too, for soon afterwards his friend Tosaki reports that the lemon cure had proved successful, and that recovery was complete. Once more Hokusai, so sorely tried by poverty and worry, gathered himself together for another great achievement which resulted in his bequeathing to posterity the gift of his *Fugaku Hakkei*, in three volumes—the 100 Fuji pictures which are, apart from the *Mangwa*, Hokusai's most popular work.

His preface to the first edition (black and grey) clearly indicates the views he then held:

"Since the age of six I have painted a great variety of objects. At 50 I had already published a prodigious series of drawings. Yet all I produced before I was 70 is unimportant. At 73 I began to understand nature, the animals, the grass, the trees, the birds, fishes and insects. At 80 I will have made further progress, and at 90 I will have penetrated into the secret of things. At 100 I shall be even better, and at 110 point and line will come to life. I ask those who live as long as myself to verify whether I keep my word. Written at the age of 75 years by myself, formerly Hokusai, today Gwakio Rojin, the Old Man Foolishly Enamoured of Drawing."

The picture series "100 Fuji" opens with a portrait of the saint of Fuji, Konohana Sakuja-hime, and a picture of the creation of the mountain. In the hundred-odd witty and jolly pictures that follow, Hokusai depicts the mountain in all possible aspects by day and night, evening and morning, summer and winter, in snow and thunderstorm. Many of these pictures range far beyond the routine even of a most gifted draftsman, and their artistic perfection has won them world fame.

A very significant sentence casting a sidelight on Hokusai's incognito existence, which had already made him a legendary figure, is contained in the publisher's preface to the third volume: "I learn that Hokusai is over 90 years of age". In reality however, Hokusai was then only 75, which seems to indicate that it was impossible even for his publisher Eirakuya to keep in direct touch with him.

Ehon Kokyo, "Filial Piety", is a work in two volumes in which the virtue of honouring one's parents is emphasized in the form of short stories. The first volume contains the humorous drawing of Ko-cleaning. The character for "filial piety", the Ko, is being brushed and burnished by youths. In the same way that we "keep our conscience clean" Hokusai shows, in his spirited manner, ten young men "keeping the Ko clean". Hokusai's book, filled with the daydreams of an ageing man, is the more touching in that the circumstances in which the painter lived were at that time sad beyond description. The husband of Hokusai's daughter from his first marriage—Hokusai was married twice—was a good for nothing, who brought great misfortune to the family. To save his son-in-law from prison Hokusai had assumed liabilities which he could not meet. In 1834 he had to flee to Uraga in the Province of Sagami and for more than five years concealed his identity under the name of Miuraya Hachiemon. Tattered and covered with lice, deprived of all means of livelihood, he lived in a shack that could not even be heated. In a letter to

HOKUSAI. *The Station Hodogaya on the Tokaido.* The Chinese character for mountain is a triangle (the mountain) which stands on a half circle, the open part turned upwards (the valley). Hokusai could not represent his beloved sacred Fujiyama more perfectly than in the form of this character. On the print therefore the mountain appears as the pure symbol itself, a triangle based on the half-circle of the upper road boundary. The same configuration is repeated in rider and horse and the group at the sedan chair. The branches of the tree are also pyramidical and form an enchanting undulating pattern, which is a repetition of the same symbol. Yet all this unreal playfulness strikes us as natural: the forest with its dark-green tops over the red stems, the tired horse with a tired horseman—nothing seems forced, nor enigmatically alien. Such a picture reveals not only consummate craftsmanship, but also the soul of a really great artist.
Signed: Zen Hokusai Iitsu hitsu. Publisher: Eijudo, Edo. 24.7 × 37.5 cm.

his publisher the old man of 78 asks for a little money. He mentions that he possesses only one coat and suffers from the cold, but at the same time he asks for paints, brush and paper, as his arm is still strong. This is followed by a number of interesting and impassioned directives regarding the production of his works. It was in such conditions as these that he created the touching *Ehon Kokyo*, in which he extols ideal historical figures such as young Sukemasa, who lost his father in battle and, while in flight and still in grave peril, wrote with his blood on the wall of the temple: "Father, you who sorrowing for me have lost your way in hell, wait, I am coming to lead you". In his radiant figures he sought to forget his own misfortunes. From time to time the old man returned secretly to Edo, a walking distance of 30 hours, in order to supervise the execution of his work at the printing works. In 1839 he came back for good, and at first hid in the temple court. "When you arrive", he wrote, "don't ask for Hokusai, as people would not know who that is. Enquire after the priest who draws there, and who lives at Gorobei's place." Hokusai painted and drew and made great plans for the future.

He bought himself a small house in Honjo whither he brought all his chattels. A fire destroyed the entire neighborhood and all his possessions went up in flames. The carefully preserved works of his younger days, his books, his sketches, his pictures, his furniture, everything was destroyed. As a mendicant, during the famine that broke out in Edo, this great man again worked his way upward. Between the age of 80 and 90 he produced the most magnificent of all his works.

One of his last publications was the "Color-book", the text of which he wrote under the name of Hachiyemon. The work was continued in a series of smaller supplementary volumes, and it was while working on one of these that Hokusai died. In instructions contained in these books, which may be considered as his artistic testament, he advises his pupils not to submit to fashionable rules but to work, like himself, in accordance only with inspiration.

Despite ninety years filled to the brim with work, poverty and sorrow he remained mentally alert, young and cheerful to the very end. His last letter to a friend reads:

"King Emma (the Prince of Hell) has reached an advanced age and intends to retire. Therefore, having had a nice country house built for himself, he now enquires whether I would be willing to paint him a *Kakemono*. Thus I am compelled to make a journey; and, when I leave, I shall take my drawings with me. I shall rent a residence at a corner of Hell Street, and shall be delighted to offer you my hospitality should you happen to pass that way. Hokusai."

Hokusai died on May 10, 1849, in the Honjo suburb, near the house in which he was born. The son of humble people, among humble people he passed away. He found them congenial; they understood him, and still revere him as one of their greatest sons.

Hokusai's work is a picture of his people, a gigantic picture such as only genius could create.

HOKUSAI. The sacred mountain appears here veiled in the smoke of an autumnal fire. The falling red maple leaves resemble shooting stars. Hokusai modestly calls this wonderful poem in images *Fuji in Smoke*. From the first volume of the "100 Fuji Pictures", 1834–1836.
Published by Eirakuya, Nagoya. 18.2 × 12.6 cm.

Next page but one. HOKUSAI. A leaf from the "100 Fuji Pictures", 1834–1836. *Storks near Fujimihagara, Owari.*
Published by Eirakuya in Nagoya. 18.2 × 12.6 cm.

烟中の不二

尾州
不二見原

162

Original study by Hokusai in Chinese ink.   31.5 × 21.5 cm.

HOKUSAI. A page from the Chinese Suiko-Den, translated and illustrated by Hokusai, published by Marukaya, 1807. *The Divine Kiu-t'ien-hünan-nü walking in the Garden of Heaven.*
18.5 × 12.5 cm.

HOKUSAI. A performance of the Kagura, the oldest religious dance of Japan, on a spring night on a terrace in the Court garden. It is still danced today at high church festivals in the Shinto temples.
The mists hovering above the Court walls and the reddish gleam of the blossoming cherry trees brighten the darkness of the night. The Court dignitaries sit in solemn array, separated from the spectators by tapestries. On the stage, two girls in voluminous garments dance the hymn to the night accompanied by the soft tunes of the flutes and drums.
Hokusai called this picture, which belongs to the series "100 Poets", *Sojo Henjo*. It is introduced by a poem which runs: "May a strong wind arise and drive away the clouds, so that we may admire a little longer the moon, the silver fairy."
Signed: Zen Hokusai with Swastika. Publisher: Yamaguchi, 1839. 25 × 37 cm.

Picture p. 166: UOYA HOKKEI (1780–1850). The fishmonger Iwabuchi was a queer fellow. He succumbed to Hokusai's spell. The noblest and most sumptuous form of the color woodcut, the Surimono, the very antithesis of his rough trade, attracted him particularly. In his mature years he took up his studies under Hokusai and became one of the greatest Surimono masters.
The New Year's greeting picture shows a poem and a temple servant in a brilliant red dress facing a bell richly decorated with copper and gold.
The signature reads: Hokkei.
Often he signed himself Uo-ya, "Fish House", or Uoya Hokkei, having in mind his fishmonger's shop. 21 × 17.7 cm.

168

KYOSAI
(1831–1889)

As a master of the woodcut he was known as Kawanabe, Shosho, Saisai, Kyosai and Gyosai.

Born at Koga in the province of Shimosa, he was apprenticed to Kuniyoshi at the age of seven. Later he joined Hokusai, but soon established himself independently. His woodcut drawings appeared in many books for which he wrote the texts and reveal a new style of painting entirely his own. His political caricatures during the time of the Shogun government earned him a prison sentence, but he was not to be discouraged and subsequently published a whole succession of further books containing satirical pictures. If proof is sought of his scholarship and serious devotion to art, it may be found in his four-volume history of art in which he reveals how intimately he knew the works of the old masters.

Subsequently he turned increasingly to pure painting and bequeathed to posterity some magnificent pictures.

Picture p. 167: KYOSAI *Raven*.
Signed: Kyosai. Red stamp Kyosai. 36.5 × 24.8 cm.

KYOSAI (1831–1889). *Basket with fishes*. From a book: Gyosai Raku Ga, Gyosai joy of drawing.
Signed: Kyosai. 18.3 × 26.4 cm.

When Tokitaro Ando, born 1797 in Edo, successfully passed his test as a master in the Utagawa clan—this was on March 9, 1812—he received the name Utagawa Hiroshige.

Little did his colleagues or his teachers suspect that this genius of fifteen was to influence European art profoundly and to open the way to Western understanding of Eastern art.

Hiroshige lived in a period of social revolution, and his life is difficult to grasp, because his prominent contemporaries gave the painter a wide berth as a revolutionary and rebel. No contemporary evaluation of Hiroshige's art is known. As a poet, however, Hiroshige had considerable success under the pen-name "Tokaido Utashige".

Tokitaro Ando was born as the son of Tokuaki Tanaka. His grandfather, Tokuyemon Tanaka, was head of the archers at the Court. The Tanakas were an old family, which had given the country a number of good soldiers. Tokuaki Tanaka, Hiroshige's father, was later adopted by the Genyemon Ando family, and his name at the birth of his son was therefore Ando.

Tokitaro Ando spent his youth in Edo near the shore, at Yayesugashi, where the Edo fire-brigade was stationed, and where his father served as an officer in the fire police. This guild of fire policemen, called *hikeshi doshin*, played an important part in the artist's life. Under the ruling Tokugawa regime, 1603 to 1867, the bourgeoisie was carefully classified, and had its duties and privileges. The *hikeshi doshin* or fire police was a form of guild; the positions, titles and rights belonged to particular families, and were heritable. Hiroshige's life was restricted to the circle of the *hikeshi doshin*. The feudal epoch had not yet ended. Edo was subject to the military dictatorship of the Shogun. The Emperor, the clerical dignitaries and the country's intellectual élite resided in Kyoto. Edo was a military and commercial city, the city of the theatres, the Yoshiwara, the tea-houses and similar places of entertainment. The members of the *hikeshi doshin* led a leisurely existence, enjoyed themselves, and lorded it over the humble folk. They produced popular singers, *Netzuke* carvers, wood-carvers and *Surimono* draftsmen, tea-ceremony masters, popular poets and craftsmen. They formed the small world of Hiroshige's parents—the world of his youth, his family, his admirers and his fame. His teachers belonged to the *hikeshi doshin* clique, as did his adopted son and son-in-law Shigenobu, and his second son-in-law, the restaurant proprietor Goto, whose name as painter was Shigemasa.

His position as brigadier of the *hikeshi doshin* enabled Hiroshige to become a river inspector, and as such to travel throughout the Tokaido (the Eastern coastal district). On these journeys he visited all the spots of his greatest and most important work "Fifty-three pictures of the Tokaido".

He is reported to have been a good draftsman at a very tender age; we know for certain that at 10 he was learning to paint under Okajima Rinsai. Both his parents died in 1809, and he inherited the post and title of a *hikeshi doshin* brigadier. Now twelve years old, his teacher, the painter Rinsai, took care of him and tried at the end of 1809 to place little Tokitaro with Toyokuni. Toyokuni, whose studio was then at the height of its fame, refused to accept the boy. Rinsai tried again later, and again unsuccessfully, to find Tokitaro a place with Toyohiro, his former colleague at the studio of the great Toyoharu. It was only at a later date that Tokitaro Ando himself was able to persuade Toyohiro to accept him. The old master had no reason to regret his decision. He was quick to recognise his pupil's outstanding gifts, took Ando into his home, and prepared him for his examinations for the degree of a master.

On March 9, 1812, the fifteen year old prodigy "Tokitaro Ando" was granted the Utagawa master-certificate. As artist he received the name of *Utagawa Hiroshige*. Toyohiro personally signed the document. The first syllable of the name Hiroshige is the last syllable in the name of his teacher.

Utagawa Hiroshige, at fifteen, now stood on the threshold of his career. For many years he worked for Toyohiro, copied, assisted in sketching, and now and then drew a picture himself. When Toyohiro died, in 1829, the Utagawa proposed giving Hiroshige the name of Toyohiro II. He declined, saying he considered himself unworthy of the great name. The real reason, however, might have been that in his heart he felt landscape painting to be his real vocation, and he therefore preferred to decline an honour which entailed responsibilities towards school and tradition.

ICHIRYUSAI HIROSHIGE
(1797–1858)

HIROSHIGE I. From the series "Eight Views from the Environment of Edo", 1832. Hiroshige calls the picture *Evening Snow at the Asukayama*. This Asuka is a hill near Edo, particularly popular in the spring when the cherry trees are in bloom. Now the alleyways, the posters, and the beloved cherry trees are hidden under the snow. The eagerness of man and beast to reach shelter accentuates the dramatic nature of the rare event. By brightening up parts of the yellowish ground Hiroshige conveys in a masterly manner the nocturnal mood and atmosphere. Signed: Hiroshige ga. Publisher: Kikakudo. 22 × 34.6 cm.

171

京都名所之内
あらし山満花

172

Meantime, Hiroshige had married the widow of a Samurai, a woman of noble descent. She bore him a son, Nakajiro. Whether it was then or at some later date that he adopted Tatsu as his daughter is not known. Temporarily transferring the post as *hikeshi doshin* officer to his uncle Ando Tetsuzo, he himself retained his position as river inspector, which enabled him to visit all the Tokaido provinces. When Nakajiro came of age, in 1833, Ando Tetsuzo resigned in his favour and thus Nakajiro became a *hikeshi doshin* brigadier. Hiroshige stayed with Toyohiro until 1829. Several pictures of birds and flowers originated in this period, to which also belongs the triptych of the giant with the green devil—and probably the *Soga Monogatari Dzuye*, several *Surimonos*, and other pieces. He painted the series "Mother and Child" in 1817.

Hiroshige's art, the art of the landscape, began only after Toyohiro's death. He reached the peak of his fame between 1831 and 1850, beginning with the work on the Tokaido sea-route.

This sea-route, 514 kilometers long, which connected Edo with the Imperial city of Kyoto, was established by Iyeyasu in the 16th century. Practically the whole later history of the island was enacted along this route. It carried the traffic between the Emperor in Kyoto and the Shogun in Edo, and served for pilgrimages, military campaigns and commerce. Small wonder that the 53 stations used for provisioning and lodging offered the artist an inexhaustible source of inspiration.

On his first art journey Hiroshige is supposed to have accompanied a deputation of the Shogun to the Emperor. The pictures of the wood engravings appeared in the same year. In 1834 these were published as a single work under the title *Tokaido Gojusan Tsugi-no Uchi*, printed by Heibei and published by Hoyaido. The Tokaido series laid the foundations of his fame among his fellow artists, friends and acquaintances.

Hitherto he had painted mainly figures, book illustrations, mythical and historical scenes, etc., which had created little interest. The Tokaido, however, brougt him wide recognition. It won him moreover two great friends, Utagawa Kunisada, nine years his senior, and the poet, painter, playwright and Ronin, Keisai Eisen, born in 1792. Both artists collaborated later with Hiroshige. Hiroshige's wife died in 1840, and his son Nakajiro in 1845. Hiroshige married again. His second wife, Yasu, was 20 years his junior, and he adopted as his heir the 19-year-old Suzuki Chinpei of the *hikeshi doshin*. He gave him as artist the name Shigenobu and took him into his home, placing him in charge of all the subsidiary work in his studio. Hiroshige had few pupils, so that Shigenobu became his main confidant. He even gave him his daughter Tatsu as wife. She, however, seems to have had very little love for the ugly, pock-marked Shigenobu and later married the young and rich proprietor of the Hyaku-Sen inn in Edo who as painter styled himself "Shigemasa".

Hiroshige had obviously succeeded in happily combining his professional journeys as river inspector with his artistic travels. This is particularly clear from his diaries, in which a thousand details are noted. He carefully records the weather, the water level, a milestone, a meal, the name of the innkeeper, and where he hails from—noting even the folk-song sung by a mendicant at the roadside.

Hiroshige created thousands of pictures which show the landscapes of old Japan. In the many Tokaido series—numerous variations on the same theme—in the Chushingura, or in the wonderful fish series, we discover a new and surprising aspect of the great master's art. There is a unique plenitude and variety in the life of Hiroshige. Despite their almost revolutionary departure from the classical concept, Hiroshige's drawings, in which contourless color surfaces replace detailed delineation, were accepted by all schools of painting from the beginning. It was Hiroshige who turned from the classical woodcut and pioneered the way to new techniques. He carried the woodcut over into a new era, so that he represents not the end of this art form but the beginning of another epoch. One of the most eminent art scholars of our time, Prof. Kenji Mariya of Tokyo, writes in his book "Japanese Painting", Tokyo 1953, "In Hiroshige's landscapes we are made aware of the self-contained world of peace which springs direct from the contemplation of nature and of the country life. His masterpieces will always represent the quintessence of Japan for the soul of the Japanese". Hiroshige died during the great cholera epidemic of 1858.

In the list of cholera victims of that year, a note following the name of Hiroshige says: Hiroshige's death is a very great loss.

HIROSHIGE I. The picture of the raftsman floating his wood down the light-blue stream past banks brimming over with the luscious blooms of spring is counted among Hiroshige's most popular pictures in Japan. The inscription reads: *Views of Kiyoto—Cherry Blossoms at the Arishi Mountain*. Signed: Hiroshige ga. Red Hiroshige stamp. Publisher: Eisendo, 1834. 22 × 35 cm.

He was buried in the inner garden of the Togaku Temple in Kita-Matsuyama-cho Asakusa, where the Ando families have their last resting place. The tombstone bears the following inscription:

HIROSHIGE. *Jumantsubo in the snow*. From Meisho Edo Hakkei: "100 views of Edo", sheet 69. Fuka-gawa, Susaki, Jumantsubo. Dated 1857. Signed: Hiroshige ga. Publisher: Uwoya Eikichi, Edo.

Ryusai Hiroshige no Haka	Ryusai Hiroshige Tombstone
Ando Yakeyo Koreo Tatsu	Erected by lady Ando
Shimizu Seifu Sho.	Placed by Shimizu Seifu.

The back of the stone is inscribed with Hiroshige's posthumous Buddhist name
Issei Genkoin Tokuo Ryusai-koji
followed by the date of his death.
The text below reads: Nisei (the second) Koryuin Ryusai Shinshi, 28th day in the 3rd month of the 27th year Meiji (1894).
The tombstone was erected by the daughter Tatsu for Hiroshige as well as for Hiroshige III.
A memorial stone for Hiroshige, with his death-song carved on it, was placed in the sanctuary of Akihajiusha in 1882. Shigemasa (Hiroshige III) reproduced it on a woodcut with the following inscription:

Azumaji-e	On the Eastland routes (in Edo)
hitsu wo nokoshite	I put down my brush
tabi no sora	Preparing myself for the journey
nishi no go-kuni no	The famous places
nadokoro wo min.	Of the Westlands to behold.

Hiroshige.

(Westland is the Paradise of Amida Buddha.)

Written by Temmei Rojin who, when he put down his brush, lifted his tear-soaked sleeves.
"The departed Ryusai Hiroshige, my teacher, was one of the best pupils of Toyo-hiro, the direct pupil of the founder of the Utagawa school, Toyoharu. He (Hiro-shige) did not study for very long under his teacher, whom he lost after 16 years. He did not seek other teachers, being ambitious to found an independent school. He therefore studied nature itself, sketched it, scaled numerous mountains and descended into many valleys. It was thus that he founded the free school for land-scapes true to nature.
Though I am an insignificant and poorish artist, yet I have inherited his name, for which reason I have endeavoured to prove worthy of him. With the kind support of Matsamoto Yoshinobu and other gentlemen, who were associated with my de-parted teacher in the field of art, I have recently succeeded in erecting before the Akiha Temple on the Sumida a tombstone with my teacher's death-song.
I am very happy that this has been possible.

Meiji XV, Year of the Horse (1882), 4th month. In reverence Ryusai Hiroshige."

175

HIROSHIGE I. In 1840 the publishing firm of Eijudo collected from several printers a series of prints representing fish and various sea animals, and published them in an album entitled *Fishes and Sea Animals*.

The poem with which Hiroshige accompanies the carp painted in various shades of grey and brown says that this fish so bravely swimming against the tide will some day ascend to heaven as a dragon. In Chinese mythology the dragon, born as a fish, rises from the water as a symbol of the spirit liberating itself from the material world. On the 5th of May, the feast of the boys, Japanese families hoist the carp flag over their homes in honour of their sons.

Signed: Hiroshige hitsu, and red stamp.

26 × 37.5 cm.

The four different Hiroshige.

The question as to whether the pictures signed Hiroshige should be attributed to the first, the second, or the third or fourth Hiroshige, has given rise to conflicting views among collectors and art historians. It appears certain that pictures dated until 1858 signed Hiroshige are the work of the first Hiroshige. Pictures dated 1858 to 1867 must be attributed to Hiroshige II, those 1867 to 1894 to Hiroshige III, and those between 1911 and 1925 to Hiroshige IV. If date and Hiroshige's seal signature are missing, only a comparison with the known pictures of the various artists allows a definite attribution. There are, however, valuable clues to be gathered from the family history of the Hiroshige.

Hiroshige I. He wrote his name in numerous ways, but the character of his signature is definitely recognizable, and has never been imitated. Utagawa Hiroshige seems the predominant signature of his early days. It was followed by Ichiryusai Hiroshige and, after 1850, Ryusai Hiroshige, in order not to be confused with the story-teller Ichiryusai Bunko.

Signatures of Hiroshige I.

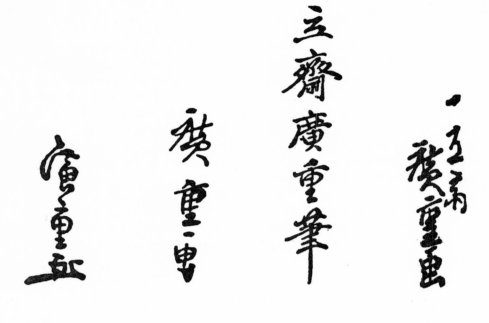

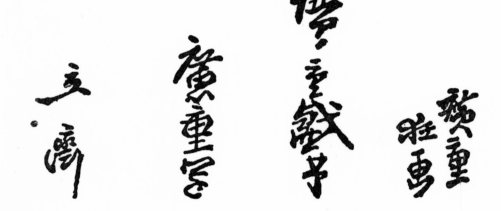

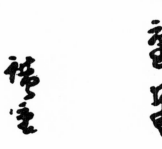

HIROSHIGE I. Hiroshige expresses the meaning of the picture of a wild duck swimming under snow covered reeds in the poem inscribed, according to an old Chinese custom, in the left-hand corner of his Hosoe:

"The wind blows over the water
And cold grips us and solitude
When the wild duck cries."

Signed: Hiroshige hitsu, followed by the red stamp. 37.5 × 17 cm.

Signatures of Hiroshige I.

To hold Hiroshige II responsible for bad pictures and attribute good pictures to Hiroshige I is wrong. Both were great artists. Hiroshige II was born in 1826, his real name being Suzuki Chinpei. He was a member of the *hikeshi doshin*. As an artist he styled himself Shigenobu, a name he kept after his adoption and until the death of the master. On pictures in which both artists had a hand we find two signatures, Hiroshige signing for the landscape and Shigenobu for the figures.

Signatures of Hiroshige II.

HIROSHIGE I. There are eight places on Lake Biwa which have been extolled repeatedly in poems and pictures. In the picture series of 1830—Hiroshige repeated the same series four times—he adds a Chinese poem to each picture. The fifth picture in the series he calls *Autumn Moon at the Ishiyama*. For at this place, once the residence of the poetess Murasaki Shibiku, the autumn moon is a particular attraction. The colors faithfully reflect the atmosphere of the moonlit night. The landscape is represented in various shades of grey on a yellowish ground. The light-blue sky darkens towards the upper margin of the picture to cobalt-blue.
Signed: Hiroshige ga, followed by the red stamp.
Publishers: Hoyeido and Eisendo.
22.5 × 44.8 cm.

180

181

182

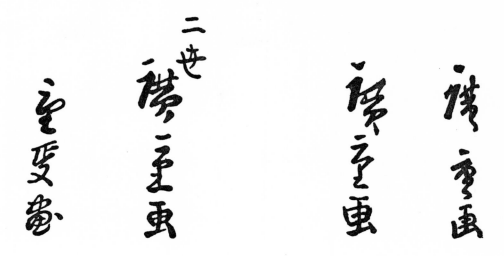

HIROSHIGE. The publisher Koshimara Heisuke arranged a book of 69 pictures by Hiroshige, which he published in 1856, in accordance with the Provinces which they represent. Hiroshige gave the book the title "Pictures of Famous Places in Japan from over 60 Provinces". Picture 42 is called *Oyashiro in the Province of Izumo* and shows the Tori-i of a Shinto Temple in the mist.
The signature reads: Hiroshige ga, in a red vignette.
34.5 × 23 cm.

The relationship between Hiroshige I and II was so intimate that it will hardly ever be possible to distinguish them with absolute certainty. All pictures bearing the Hiroshige seal and signature, and dated before 1858, the year in which he died, have to be attributed to Hiroshige I.

Several pictures from the book Meisho Edo Hakkei signed by the second Hiroshige were probably produced, apart from certain details, by the first Hiroshige, and were completed by his successor after the master's death only to permit publication of this work. After Hiroshige's death Shigenobu temporarily assumed the name "Hiroshige", and subsequently "Nisei Hiroshige". The form of the second syllable "Shige" is however definitely different from that of the first Hiroshige.

After his divorce from his wife Shigenobu lived in seclusion. He worked first with Okajima Rinsei, married a second time, and associated himself with his teacher's friend, Kunisada. In the ninth volume of the Yehon Edo Miage, 1864, he still signs himself "Hiroshige". In the 10th volume, published 1867, he signs himself "Sakino Hiroshige Rissho", meaning Hiroshige changed to Rissho. In the same year Japan arranged an exhibition of his pictures at the Paris exhibition. During the stormy days of the Meiji revolution he was quickly forgotten, and while the art dealers of France, Britain and the United States were making big money by the discovery of Hiroshige II, the artist himself died, aged only 44, impoverished and forsaken, in 1869.

Hiroshige III, born in 1842 at Futagawa as the son of a shipwright, was called Goto. As a pupil of Hiroshige he styled himself Shigemasa. Later, after being adopted by the proprietor of the Hyuaku-Sen inn, he married the daughter of Hiroshige, divorced from Shigenobu. He is supposed to have assumed the name "Hiroshige II", or simply "Hiroshige", in 1867. No great works by him are known. Like his father-in-law, who once collaborated with Kunisada I, he joined the second Kunisada. Not an important artist, he was pre-eminently known as the proprietor of Edo's best restaurant, and the heir of his famous father-in-law's name. Hiroshige III died in 1894.

Hiroshige IV, born 1848, and called Kikuchi-Kiichiro, was a pupil of Shigenobu, and at the age of 63 was awarded the honour of the "Hiroshige" name. He endeavoured to revive the declining art of landscape painting with the help of woodcuts in the old style. He died in Tokyo in 1925, aged 77.

HIROSHIGE. *The Vortex of Naruto in the Province of Awa* represents the 55th sheet in the picture book "Pictures of Famous Places in Japan from over 60 Provinces". The deep-blue breaker with its foam is reminiscent in color and design of Hokusai's "Wave", undoubtedly known to Hiroshige. The two pictures cannot, however, be compared as there is a basic difference between them. Hokusai's work has a profound meaning, whereas Hiroshige's picture is pure play, however charming in color and form.

Signed: Hiroshige ga, in a red vignette. Publisher: Koshimura Heisuke. 34.5 × 24

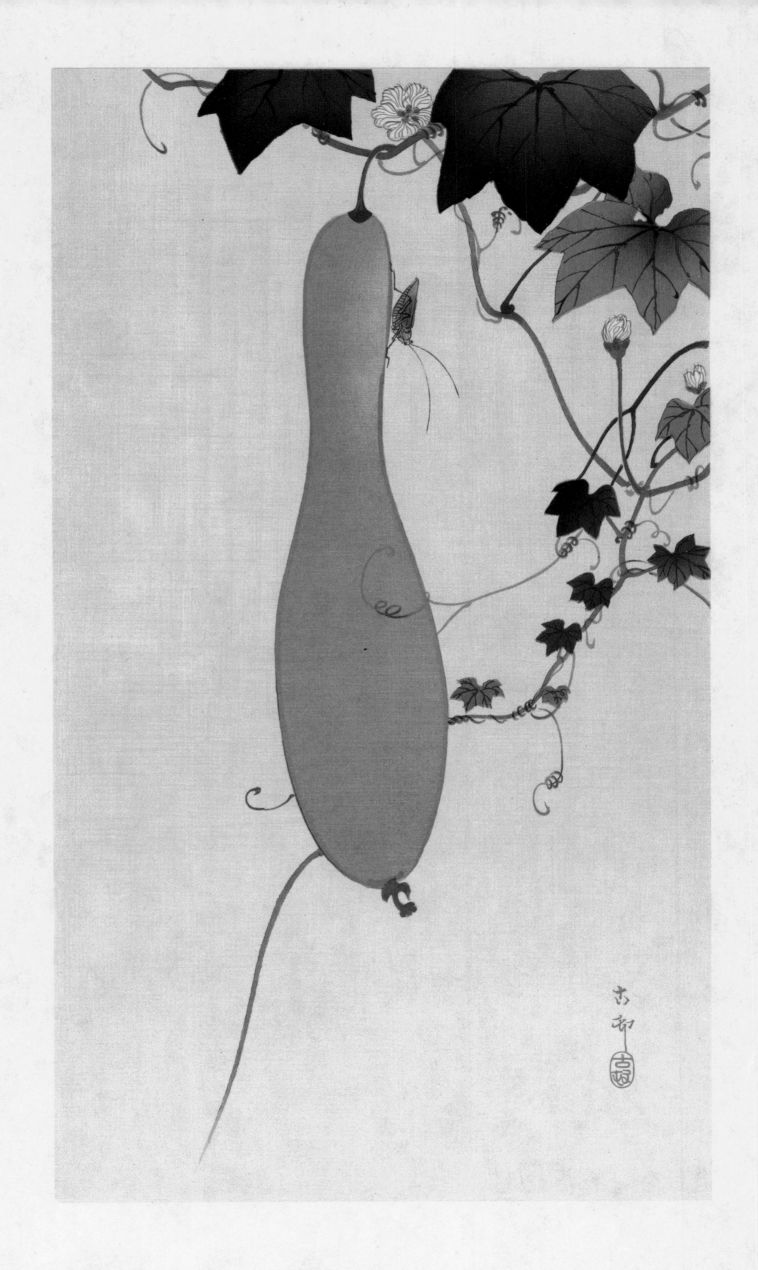

OHARA KOSON
(1877–1945)

later Shoson, with the civil name Matao, came from Kanazawa, Province of Kaga. He was a pupil of Suzuki Kason in Tokyo. The Spanish American, Fenollosa, professor at the Imperial university and teacher at the School of Art in Tokyo had great influence on the young artist's work. Koson specialized in flowers and birds. He signed with the name Koson. His publisher was Daihei Ryogoku. After 1912 he dedicated himself entirely to brush painting and from then on called himself Shoson. In 1926 he found the way back to wood-cutting. His publisher at this time was Watanabe, signature Shoson. He is the typical exponent of the modern woodcut, who carries on the tradition of his predecessors without being influenced by other non-Japanese conceptions of art. Ohara Koson died in Tokyo in 1945.

Picture p. 186: KOSON. *Blossoms in the moonlight.*
34.5 × 18.8 cm.

Preceding color print: KOSON. *Tendril.*
34.5 × 18.8 cm.

187